The Saxon saga and other poems

William Turberville

BIBLIOLIFE

THE SAXON SAGA

AND OTHER POEMS

CONTENTS

	PAGE
HYMN TO THE SPIRIT OF POETRY . . .	I
THE SAXON SAGA	7
POEMS OF IMAGINATION—	
Love in the Universe . . .	113
Love in the Earth	121
To God (by a nature-taught modern)	123
To God (by a culture-killed modern)	128
God—A Child's Song . . .	129
Nature's Song	130
Winter's Come !	130
My Soul . . .	132
The Sceptic Veil . . .	148
The Future Life	149
To a Lily of the Valley . . .	150
The Light of Death	151
This Crown of Thorns . .	154
Emotion, Written and Spoken .	154
To my Brother, on my Mother's death	155
The New-born Century	157
Beauty in Loving-Kindness .	158
A Tribute to the Rev. Dr Momerie . .	159
Saint Paul's	161
The Spell	164
To Mr T. H.	168
To the Same	168

Contents

PAGE

Three Sonnets on the Future Life . 169
An Exhortation to the Anglo-Saxon . 171
The Human Cry 171
To a Mother 172
Life's Sullied Heritage 173
The Garden of White Flowers . . 179
Tell me, Little Sparrow ! . . 182
My Discarded Body 184
Invocation to Spring . . 187
To the Unknown Proprietor of a Wood marked
  " Private, Trespassers will be Prosecuted " 195
Late Spring . . . 197
Nature one with my Soul in Springtime 197
Song of a Heart of the City . 198
Song of a Heart of the Country 200
Music at Death . . . 203
Baby Enchanting . . 204
Sympathy 205
The Yearning for Perfection . 206
A Word 207
The Wedding of Goodness and Happiness . . 208
Charles Edward Troughton . . 209
O Strange World . . . 210
Man, an Instrument Used or Abused 211
The War of Life . . . 211
The Blessings of Forgetfulness 212
To Poetry 213
Rich and Poor (the rich man to the poor man) 214
Rich and Poor (the poor man to the rich man) 215
Youth and Age (age to youth) . 217
Youth and Age (youth to age) 217
The Years Creep on, the Cruel Creeping Years . 218
Blighted Spring . 218

Contents

	PAGE
To Autumn .	223
The Sword's Question	223
To the *Hypocritical* Boer	224
The Boer War	225
The Dying Ottoman	226
The Empire Psalm .	227
Peace !	229

LOVE POEMS—

The Song of the Rose-lily-Fair	233
Love has Come !	247
To Maiden Innocence	248
"Good-bye"	249
Love, My Guest	250
So Fair, so Fond !	252
Life and I	253
Had ever Lover a Love like Mine ?	254
To My Love	256
The Zephyr of Love	256
To My Love	257
A Question of Love	257
A Bachelor's Complaint	258
He Came and Went	259
My Lady of Beauty	259
Love's Resurrection	260
My Lady Fair	262
My Lady Frail	264
May I call my Loved One "Mine"?	265
Young Love's Eternity	266
Mother ! Mother ! a Maid's Appeal	267
Wedding Bells	270
As Down Life's Stream I Flow	271
The Ballad of the Lily-White-Hand	273

Contents

	PAGE
Lilia . .	274
Longing for Rest	275
When She Smiles .	276
When My Lady Sings .	277
To a Heart Suppressing Sweet Love	279
Song . . .	280
My Lady's Hidden Sun .	281
My Lady's Lily .	281
Love's Passion .	282
Love's Appeal to Nature	284
Mated but Loveless . . .	284

HYMN TO THE SPIRIT OF POETRY

1.

My Childhood saw thee sleeping 'mid the stars,
　Large wonder in mine eyes,
While God in silence drove those silver cars
　Across His skies.

2.

With thee I saw the scented, pale blue-bell
　Peer through dead leaves of gold,
And heard the gentle tale it had to tell,
　Each year retold.

3.

With thee I listened to romanceful rills
　And hollow sprites in caves,
Soft voices of the woodlands and the hills,
　Wild, sobbing waves,

4.

'Till, wooed by Night and the impassioned seas,
　Star-magic in the air,
I fell with thee upon my bended knees
　Enrobed in prayer.

2 Hymn to the Spirit of Poetry

5.

Then with thy mind I read the Book of Youth,
  Love hidden in the leaves,
And from its tales I gleaned the wondrous Truth
  That Love conceives.

6.

And I have seen thee by blind Homer sit
  Thought-picturing his brain,
'Till lovely Helen and Ulysses' wit
  Lived o'er again.

7.

Through the dim vista of my sensuous dream
  Thy love-lit spirit glows,
Like a wild sun-set glory, flecked with cream
  And flushed with rose.

8.

With thee I conjure ages that have been
  Since playwright Time began
To act upon this daily shifting scene
  His play of Man.

9.

And I have seen thee gaze with prophet-eye
  'Till in effulgent birth
Beneath thy sacred muse of majesty
  Rose a new earth,

10.

And chariotted to Heaven by steeds of fire
  'Neath the Creator's throne,
Thou hast, all throbbing with divine desire
  For the Unknown,

11.

Lifted into a holier, purer air,
  This sorrow-stainèd sphere,
From all its feverish fens of fretful care,
  And sin-fed fear.

12.

Thou wondrous Spirit! touch me, move me, speak!
  Lead me to heights with thee,
'Till in the sunrise, on some magic peak
  My mind shall see!

THE SAXON SAGA

THE SAXON SAGA

CANTO I

ENGLAND, my country! if thy statesmen bold
Dare chasten thee, why may not I, thy slave,
Thy lover, thy devoted son, speak words
Into thine ear? For I am old and gray
With toil of thought, and would thee gently woo
With wisdom of my years, before I pass
Into the mystic Silence. Not that I
Deem I have yet attained; alas! alas!
I still behold the highest wisdom-peak,
Towering above me in the distant blue,
Snow-clad, and crystal-pure, and rainbow-hued,
Far from my feeble footsteps. Yet, I hope!

Forgive me if, I, angry with the world,
Use no vain, delicate, deceitful words,
But choose plain Saxon, frozen by the North
Into the pure transparency of Truth.

Forgive me, too, if I should weakly fail
To move thee with the mission of my mind;
But ever let the good intention be
My plea for utterance.
Oft feel I like some searcher for the Pole,
Whose hope doth buoy him through a frozen sea,
So great my task, so scant my frosted breath
To sound my dream abroad.
But I have seen the Vision in the sky;
Watched mountains move, and rivers pause in fear
While the dread secrets of the Deep were bared.

And I have heard weird Voices in the air ;
The deep-toned Oracle within my soul ;
The priestly chantings of the sacred Sea
Washing its wailful waves round sin-stained man.
How can I then keep silence !
I, who have dreamed, throbbing with Time's great
    heart,
My mind, like some astrologer's of old,
Viewing the destinies of half mankind
Writ in the stars of heaven !   Whose eye beholds
A field of golden Ruin, where the stacks
Of columned coins glittering in the sun,
Draw forth no tender heart to wail or sing :
A sordid field, dead as Sahara's dust !
At which my flesh hath shudder'd in despair,
Looking for green leaves, moist with sap of Spring,
And throbbed with God's great heart.   Ah ! how my
    soul,
Bathed in an overwhelming flood of awe,
Has feared to look upon the eye of Day
As my imaginative gaze beheld
Phalanx 'gainst phalanx, man 'gainst brother man
Hurling their wondrous forms into the grave,
That those who live, may, glorying, filch away
A little plot of earth, or some mean gain,
That never can be measured with a man :—
Lo ! a loved martyr for a noble cause
In the white scales of Heaven lifts a star !
Ah ! it is passing strange ;
So little wisdom, and such floods of gore !
So black man's frowning morn,
And yet such streams of Light from smiling Heaven !
Oh ! then, my Country, tune me to my song !

The Vision came to me on Christmas Eve
When bells were pealing forth through London streets
Their tidings great with joy :—" Glory to God ;

Peace on the earth ; good-will from Heaven to man ! "
The muffled snow made silent all the ways
So that the taleful tongues of the sweet bells
Thrilled everywhere; save when their charm was broke
By hoarse-voiced Christmas revellers rolling home
Meandering with their wine, while souls, more staid,
Woke frighted from their beds to sigh for sleep.
Locked was my door, and in the frosty fire
I drew strange fancies, such as gently creep,
Silent as feathery fairies in a brain,
I seemed to see the hammer of God's wrath
On a dread anvil breaking sordid souls,
And Shadrach, Meshach, and Abednego,
Walking before the pride of Babylon
With the Ethereal Fourth, entranced my gaze ;
Then saw I burning Hope fall from the fire,
Changed to a blackened cinder of Despair ;
'Till a white figure through the close-shut door
Glided before me, and I paused and feared.
His face was white as marble, clear as glass,
But, unlike marble, it seemed strangely warm,
And kind it was and brightly beautiful,
And his large, lustrous, dreamful, yearning eyes
Drew my worn spirit from my throbbing flesh
And led me, disembodied, where they willed ;
While my frail fingers, with a fertile pen
Silently wrote all the grand scenes I saw.

He touched me, and with wooing wisdom said :—
" I am thy Country's Spirit ; in my hand
Her Destinies I hold, and I will show
To him who loves me, wonders of the Past
And marvels yet to come ! " Thus, all inflamed
With such grand promise, on my knees I fell,
And faintly uttered to that starlike form
My meek submission :—
" Let me, Oh ! Spirit, Follow, See, and Hear ! "

Then, as an eagle gathers to his breast
His fascinated prey, with spirit-wings
He bore me through the walls, o'er glimmering lights,
Lining the empty streets ; o'er sleeping fields
Warmed by the woolly snow ; o'er towers and spires,
And solemn outlines hid 'neath Night's dusk arms ;
Until he seemed to lose control of air
And helpless fell o'er the round rim of earth
Into a deep, dark space of empty gloom !
(Here was my soul with higher sense endowed.)
Then, nearing earth, we saw the eastern shores
Of our loved land, by boisterous billows stormed,
Pounding the shingle into grains of sand.
And, as we gazed, the sun peeped slowly forth
Around a crimsoned corner of the world,
And through a cloudy curtain lit the sea.
There saw we multitudes of tossing barks,—
Mere baby vessels bruised in Neptune's arms—
Blown by an Eastern tempest towards the land.
Strong, blue-eyed men, with flowing, flaxen hair,
Guided the helms, or clung to slippery prows,
Without a flinch of fear ;—their one desire
To be upon a crested billow borne,
(Tho' shocked, and bruised, and faint,) to British
    ground

" Who are these daring mariners," I asked,
" That seem to seek their Glory in their Death ? "

" They are thy country's Ancestors," said he,
" The Viking brood, martyrs to truth and speed,
Who nerve thine arm with strength, thy soul with
    fire ,
Behold ! as their frail vessels touch thy shore
How quick they are to mend their overthrow !
They shout defiance to the drowning waves,
Call on their gods to help them, mount the beach,

And from the drowning thousands, thousands save.
The wind of God came with them ; born were they
To found the longed-for Empire of the Free.
See ! in the woods, with look of sullen scorn,
The uncohesive Kelt,
Brave as his conquerors
But not composed of stuff to grip the world ;
More neatly snared in network of soft words,
Captured by glamour, praise, and sweetened lies,
Looking for Fortune in a lap of dreams,
Fair, fond, deluded, daring, restless, blind,
But loved by all.
And yet the Kelt shall lift the Saxon soul,
Like the upheaving leaven in the flour,
And both shall praise me with the heart-born song."

At this his voice into the silence died,
And I beheld, in wonder, myriad wings
Fluttering from far,
'Till like a serried army in the sky
They walled us round ; a throng of angels white
Encanopied in blue,
And o'er each angel's forehead stood a star.
These were the spirits born in ages past,
Life of the dust of nations, who had writ
Their story on the earth, and then had fled
With buoyant Hope into the mystic gloom.
Spirits from farthest Ind, where the hot breath
Of an eternal Summer 'laxed the limbs
And steeped the brain in dreams, and nursed the soul
To slumber in a calm, serene Despair.
And stronger souls were there from frozen North,
Who fought for Life numbed by Despondency,
Resting their flesh upon the white-wool-snow,
When in the faint of Death they watched for Dawn
O'er earth's keen, ice-clad pinnacles, made rich
With diamond-stars. Ah ! all were there who thought

Or stormed against the world, and helped to lift
Their brothers into Light,—Great satirists
Of ages dead, whose stricken hearts had flayed
Their friends with words!   Countless beginnings they,
And countless endings, too, of tortured thought
Born in the mind of Man ; the very cream
Of earth's nobility.   Towards them all I yearned.
Then, like the twilight blushing to the morn,
I saw a bloom spread o'er the serried throng,—
The bloom that blushed o'er Eden when frail man
First looked un-innocent upon the world ,
And a great sound of Music reached my ears
As though God waked Heaven's richest harmonies
Upon the soul of man.   The prelude ceased,
And from the serried throng this anthem rang :—

"We who have delved in earth, and fled to heaven,
Solving the mystery of the human mind,
Fall down before thy newly-fashioned Form,
And on thee shower our blessing and our love.
All that our hearts have gleaned on land or sea
We now impart to thee.   Search not for us
In dull scholastic leaves ; for some knew not
The magic of the pen, but, green with Spring,
And tenderly impressed with Nature's thought,
Heard with entrancing Memory the Godhead play
The deep-toned organ of the Universe
We are thy strong fore-runners and to thee
We bring our best and brightest , all our Thought
Born in those far-off centuries when Man
Lived in eternal earth, and saw no more
Than the revealing sun, 'till Truth upsprang
In mystic Babylon, where the sweet stars
First spake their wonders, and our eyes discerned
God moving in the sky : in Egypt, where
Man first controlled the waters, and grew skilled
In laws and principles that balance worlds

Without supporting finger in the blue ;
In Greece, where golden emulation bade
Man pierce the clouds that shadow the Sublime ;
Where Æschylus, lit with Promethean fire,
Saw the weird working of eternal Truth ;
Where the dead marble woke to dreams of life
At the skilled touch of famed Praxiteles,
Who taught the flying flutter of a dress
To the rude stone : in the Celestial world,
Where great Confucius moral mountains climbed
Above his valleyed fellows 'till he touched
The hand of God, and lived to see Him smile :
In Persia, where the Zoroastrian dream
Had led the Magi to the Bethlehem star ;
In Rome, whence grew thè conquerors of the world,
And Man first taught his brother to be free :
And deeper still
In that Great Book where Hebrew bards inscribed
The Visionary Presence, ere to the blue
They fled for earth's Redeemer.   Take our best
And mould it with thy strength, that we may live
Our higher motives once again in thee ! "

I felt my Guide thrill with this choral strain,
And, as it ceased, the mighty multitude
Fled like a mist away.
            "But," said I,
"Where, where is he who beamed upon our world
The sun of Love, and made us garments fair,
For courtly entrance to the realms on high ? "
"Wait!" said my Guide, "these are the souls who soared
Ere the good Christ endowed the world with wings ! "

So o'er the earth he floated, like a star
Jewelling the golden armour of the morn,
When, suddenly, from every point in heaven,
Dazzling my spirit-eyes, came wonderous rays

Converging to the earth, 'till through its core
We saw the solar sun just issuing forth
Beyond earth's rim, and the dull earth became
An airy bubble floating in the blue,—
For 'neath those rays base Matter changed to Naught,—
And where they centred in the bubble-earth
We saw the Great Magician of our World,—
The Saviour whom our brutal hands had slain
Because He shed Heaven's light on man's loved lies,
There was His face,—His calm, grave, earnest face—
Looking in pity on the Universe,
With just a rising brightness in His eyes
As though fair Hope was floating thro' His gaze.
" List ! " said my Guide, " He will the heavens enchant
With magic words.   Behold how Silence reigns
In sun, and earth, and moon, and listening stars ! "

Then came a sound more dulcet than the ear
Of daily earth has known ; more sweet than tongue
Of love-lorn lady lilting to her love
When roams his heart afar ; more soft and strange
Than echoed music voiced by sleeping hills
'Neath night's deep blue ; more tender-true than tears
Heart-welled in grief ; more soothing than the fall
Of wailing waters wandering to the sea :
Words fail to colour clear the tender tones
That wooed the spirits in the halls of Space :—

" Spirits who love this World where I was Love,
Who fondly hope to see Man's royal race
Raised to the throne of God, behold the hour
When from this sea-locked land I conjure forth
The unspoil'd Saxon, Jute, and Angle brave,
With hearts made proof against adversity,
To do my will.   Freely my heart forgives
My own rude race who forced on Me the crown
Of cruel thorns (for, ere I came, they sang

Some music of God's mind,) but now I choose
My champions from the North to build a Throne
Among the nations, where my Thought shall flame
For ever as a sacrificial fire
Unto the teeming multitudes to come,
And Man shall know that it were best to die
Than stand on Earth a traitor to Love's creed!"

And as these words rolled echoing thro' the clouds
That robed the firmament, my Guide and I
Throbbed with delight, as though the yearning voice
Spake like ourselves, and were a part of us;
At which I, wondering, said:—
                "Guide of my life,
This voice doth seem an echo of my soul;
Oft did I hear it when with baby-mind
I gazed on Life through the young eyes of Dream,
It seems to me like daisies in the mead,
Like green trees 'gainst the blue, like stars in heaven,
Like sunshine on a rose—the very breath
And poetry of Life,—and yet, I fear."

"Thy soul is but expanding," said my Guide,
Man sees but goodness at his first fair peep
At this loved world,
But, like a Vandal, he destroys the scene,—
The priceless treasure,—'till his slaughtering hands
At last are cleansed by Death, when, with wild fear
Man tears the veil aside, and looks Beyond!
Thou shalt see greater depths and heights
Than these, if thou to Nature and thyself be true,
And show to touch of Love no cold-eyed scorn."

At these good words I calmed; 'twere vanity
To scoff at my own feelings, as too oft
Doth flippant Man in witty epigram,
Treating his life as an unconscious stone
Tossed by a sportive child into the sea!

But I was hurried out of brooding thought
By a strange voice that passed from world to world
Like chords of thunder heard among the clouds ;
At which I turned, enquiring, to my Guide.

" It is a magic utterance from Heaven," he said,
"Some mandate flashed by the Almighty Will
From star to star, heard not by Earth's deaf ears."
And, as he spake, we dropt into Earth's air
And felt the muffled silence hush the spheres.
Then said my Guide :—
" Behold how Man's wild spirit tortures Earth :—
At Rome sit troubled Cæsars, weak with fears,
Watching their world-famed empire claim the dust,
As the bold Goth batters the fabric down !
The Saracen, girt with Mahomet's sword,
Breaks thro' the walls of fair Jerusalem ;
But these wild Angles, heedless of all fear,
Shall feel no Roman yoke, and ape no tongue,
But as the Godhead made them aye remain.
Ah ! Rome, Rome, Rome ! mother of nations thou !
How swiftly rose thy sun from Tiber mists
Draped in empurpled splendour ; and how soon
It faded in a night of a gloom ; how soon
False Pleasure sapped thee,—stole thy soul
And tossed it withered in the way of Life !
Yet didst thou, in thy moment, light mankind
To Alpine heights of Beauty, Love, and Truth ;
In thy right hand a sword, and, in thy left,
The scales of Justice weighing righteous laws !
This new-born race shall never fail as thou,
But a perennial freshness o'er the land
Shall bid her roses bloom, and raise her corn,
And keep alive her faith in Love and Truth !"

Even as his voice subsided forth there rose
A trumpet call from Rome, and we beheld

The steel-clad legions march from Adrian's wall
Fear-struck, yet hungering for the burning South
To fight the strong barbarians nearer home,
'Till not a Roman languished in our land.
Then Saxon vied with Saxon ; from the East
Fleet after fleet with mighty men appeared
For conquest born, 'till from Northumbria's gates.
To wooded Kent a mighty avalanche
Of Saxon strength, bruising the tender fields,
Drove the bewildered Kelt to watch the sun
Fall in soft glory 'neath the silent hills
That guard the gates of Wales.   Day after day
The sun was bathed in blood and boded war.
Fierce grew the heart of man ; the air was rent
With cries of innocents, and none could stem
The stream of blood that rivered through the land.

Then my strange Guide led me a century on,
And showed me how the Keltic fringe had shrunk
To a thin streak along the Western shore ;
While the brave Saxon, glowing with his pride,
Strove for the over-lordship, tribe 'gainst tribe.
Then I beheld a tumult in the heavens ;
Millions of Angels flocked from every sphere
And hovered o'er our Isle, for 'twas a day
When Light and Darkness fought for mastery.
The Sacred Cross, electrified from Heaven,
Was borne from tribe to tribe by tonsured priests
Robed in fine chasuble, or alb, or stole,
Or vestments holy ; thane after thane fell down
And worshipped, but the grovelling, lower mind,
Firm-fixed in heathendom, felt not the spell
Of Earth's new Lord, and in their hearts rebelled,
'Till Pagan Penda, scorning those who preached
And never practised what their Christ had taught,
Rose,—heathen to the last,—and slew with zeal
The band of proselytes who stormed his realm

B

Not for Christ's Love but all for greed of gold !
Then saw I Peter, saint of purpled Rome,
Sweep down from star-land, beckoning to his side
The multitudes of souls that filled the sky.
"Spirits of Earth !" the Apostle's voice proclaimed,
" The heathen triumph in this chosen land,
The vales rejoice in Frida, Woden, Thor,
And Christ is trampled under foot of man.
Oh ! why will man ne'er hear the voice that calls
Unto his inner ear in silent song ;
Why will he worship beauty of the eye
And reverence not the beauty of his mind,—
Purity, Honour, Holiness, and Truth ?
Let us exalt these chosen souls to heights
Untrod before by man ; let Love inspire
Some burning tongue to voice immortal thought,
Honeyed with eloquence, that this grand race
May cast its heathen dreams into the Past
And worship God alone ! "
Then all the angels formed a mighty Cross
That stretched from North to South o'er all the land,
And there they sung a supplication sweet.
But never Saxon saw that wondrous sight
Amid the stars,—'twas not for earth-born eyes,
Yet when he tilled the sobbing ground next morn,
Perchance he thought such copious floods of dew
Were not the nightly gems that drop from heaven,
But rain of angel-tears, made large with Love,
Shed o'er his heathen soul, and not in vain.
For as my Guide and I hung in the heavens,
We felt the holy rays of God pour down
Upon the stricken land, even as the sun
Rouseth the trees and flowers to spring-tide life,
And forth, through all the people, God-like dreams
Flowered from their daily toil, and Christ became
Not a mere emblem, but a living Truth
That struck the aged, heathen Penda down.

Then saw we some great artist paint in blood
A mystic battle on Northumbria's plains,
Where Christian fought with heathen round the Cross,
And priests, wild-chanting warlike litanies,
Sign the Red-Cross over the Christian slain.
A lurid scene of fire and floods of wrath,
'Mid fluttering silken banners, lit by Heaven
With rays from God, as all the heathen host
Flying in fear were in great waters drowned

Then saw I Peter dip his hand in blood
And write upon the firmanent God's will —
"England from henceforth shall My Son adore!"
(While Plato gazed in silence on the scene,)
And a white angel-choir in triumph sang :—
      "Thor with his thunder
      Like a day's wonder
           Passeth away;
      Christ with love-story,
      Giving God glory,
           Bringeth the Day!"
Then said I to my Guide ;—"It seemeth strange
That God should plant on this small plot of earth
His chosen few to mirror to the world
The love of Truth through all the fleeting years,
When learned hands have built in lovelier climes
Bewildering temples of philosophy,
That tower amid the clouds and glisten fair
In the gold sunbeams."
                And at this my Guide
Turned to me with reproachful eyes and said ;—
"Man knoweth not the mystery of Life ;
He builds philosophies on moving sands,
Or on the ice of Reason which dissolves
'Neath suns of Love. His theories but hold
The misty empire of his little mind,
While Earth calls loudly from a thousand tongues

For greater light than one small mind can glean.
Therefore God wrapped this land in swaddling clothes,
Sweeping the old, worn, human past away;
Waking the moral force anew in man,
So that the mighty lung of this strong race
Shall shout injustice down and tyrants dare!"

CANTO II

As early man of earth's foundations dreamed
Ere the great sun proclaimed its place in heaven
To his dull mind, so, on these wonders, I
In ignorance gazed; then questioned I my Guide :—
"Whence come these pictures of the Past? And how
Canst thou enkindle at thy will dead fires
Of human thought?" To which he deigned reply :—
"Stupendous archives in the ether hold
In spirit forms all memories of Life;
(Not as with man, who, in material books,
With his proud pen inscribes his conscious mind;)
Thus every action done and every thought
Are kept by powers unseen for future eyes,
And I unfold unto thy new-born mind
How round the earth the myriad spirits play,
How world responds to world, and all are held
In the wise palm of one o'ermastering Hand!
Man looks on earth and sees the gentle Spring
Bud forth from Winter's breast, hears Summer's hymn
Die into Autumn's dirge, and deems Life's dream
Of Time-worn Matter born! Caged in his town
He bargains with himself, and shuts from view
Thought's wide sublimity! In the deep sky
He finds eternal Silence, though he longs
For spoken word! Ah! blind and deaf is he!
The song that charmed Creation in him sings,
The spirit of the ages in him breathes,

And leaps and quivers with eternal fire ! "
At this my lips were silent, and I clung
Close to his side in fear, for I was dazed
With this large view of life.   My mind, indeed
Had crept into my flesh, but now I saw
A new expanding vision meet my gaze.
The passion of my people filled my soul,
I lived not for myself but for a cause :
So as the fiery meteors swept my side
I felt their haste, as they their missions bore
From God's great throne to distant hierarchies.
And I was friendly with the hurrying moon
As round the earth she bore her ministry
Of Light to man.   And I would e'en have been
Like them, a humble messenger of Truth.
Fain would my mind have shown my brother-man
How individual manhood levers Earth
Nearer the throne of God ; and how earth-dense
Was pious Milton, when with mighty voice,
Like a grand organ pulsing sacred sounds,
He sang of Satan casting at God's throne
The gauntlet of rebellion : as though God,
Who tossed the stars from His creative Hand
Could brook such puny plots against His power.
As well conceive a fly could flutter man
With buzz of war !   No armoured Satan here
Lifted his sword 'gainst Heaven ; to me it seemed
As though Death cleansed each soul in his cold stream
Before the flight for God, so pained Heaven's eyes
To see Man stain his soul with wanton hands !
There was no sign of one rebellious star
Daring the God of worlds ; but all was law
And an eternal harmony of Mind.
Yea ; I know well
That He who made the governing laws of Life,
Who reared sweet Reason in Man's magic brain,
Made each fair Truth with its black Opposite,

With Height,—Depth ; with Beauty,—Hideousness ;
With Goodness,—Evil ; but no daring Form
E'er strode into the Vast with damaged mind
And wrote upon his brow a lie to God :—
" Behold in me,—Evil Personified ! "
Moved by these thoughts, quick flooding o'er my
    brain,
I said to my kind Guide : " Behold ! our race
Are but to butchery born ; tribe against tribe,
Brother 'gainst brother striveth for control :
All the sweet woodland flowers are fringed with gore
While in the heavens I see sad spirit-eyes
Weep for such Cain-born souls, who give no place
To gentle precedence, but rise and slay
All that opposeth their tumultuous will ;
Tell me, doth Justice rule ? "   To which my Guide,
Sad at man's earthly tendency, replied :—
" Who can explain the brute that lives in man ?
A mortal ever robes himself in scorn,
But, as the Godhead wills, so must it be :
From storms of trial, springs the conquering soul.
Mark, in these scenes of blood, how Courage stands
With hot flushed face before Death's archery ;
How naught but strength strides o'er the conquered
    field !
So that from sinewy ancestors we rise
A race made strong to helm the storm-tossed world.
See how in Wessex great King Alfred reigns
And lifts his people from the thrall of war
Into the heaven of thought, while round his Court
His serried armies fend away the foe,
Mark how his tiny navy rides the waves,—
The hundred fathers of the British fleet
That now doth guard the Seas of all the world
From pirate plunder.   Slowly groweth man !
How many generating hands decayed
Ere happy fingers charmed the waiting reed

Into the warbling flute ! How many lips
Blew thro' that trembling reed the trivial tune
Ere a divinity upon it breathed
And in the throbbing orchestra of life
Drew forth the sacred music of the Soul !
How many Adams gazed across the foam
Ere one high-priest of Science rose to wed
The flirtful canvas to the wooing breeze
And sailed away amid derisive eyes !
The eagle's flight into the silent heaven
Is but a lesson newly learnt by man !
But yesterday he caged the lightning-flash
And stored the vapours' hidden majesty,
Although the earth has borne his easy mind
Ten thousand busy circles round the sun !
Oh, then be not impatient with thy race !
In fruitful time the perfect few shall spread
Till strength, unyielding, sineweth the land ;
And, with the strength, the everlasting roots
Of tender flowers shall thread their silent way
'Gainst bitter gardener Winter's ruthless plough,
Or cloud-wrapt Summer's desolating tears ;
For from this field of Life the world shall glean
Wild flowers of Courage, passion-flowers of Faith,
Rose-buds of Beauty, hawthorn-boughs of Hope,
And orange blooms of Chastity, entwined
In honey-suckle Love-bonds ; posy sweet
To be in laurel-crown of Glory framed.
Be not cast down, when, 'scribed upon the Past,
Ye see how those who lifted Thought to heaven
Have lazily into inertia swooned ;—
Babylon, Memphis, Thebes and Nineveh,
And Dian's Ephesus, on which the dust
Has fallen gently, while man's besom dreamed.
Here all man's complex energies, made free,
Shall never falter in the flight to come.
But see ! e'en yet the pangs of travail spread."

Then from our breathless altitude we fell
Below a pall of clouds, which, in the sun,
Gleamed like a fleecy veil of billowy white,
Flung over modest earth in flowing folds.
But 'neath the floating veil all drear it was,
Sunless and hopeless, like a murderer's fear ;
How oft, like this, I felt man's face had lied
With flowery smile above a heart of scorn !

Far in the distance in the gray-clad sea
We saw from every point frail Viking boats
In danger tossed, torn by a wind that blew,—
Like the last trumpet, portents great with wrath ;
And each frail boat fine freights of valour bore
To our loved land.   All round the eastern coast
Like a destroying pestilence they fell.
"The Danes, the Danes !"   I heard the Saxon's cry!
Out sprung the sword, and yet the cruel Dane
Landed and fought, wooing the cherished ground ;
And far and wide we saw blood, fire, and smoke,
Mingled with cries of anger blown in blasts
From soul-stirred man !   Only the mighty lived !
Never a coward laughed in sight of heaven
And slyly slid behind his conqueror.
It was a day that searched all trembling flesh :
Majestic winnowings flung the coward soul
Like chaff afar !   Strength, only strength prevailed !
"Is this the work of God ?" I asked my Guide.
"Yea," said his voice. "Lightly he treateth Flesh ;
The puny buildings of primeval man
Disperse like vapoury clouds and naught remains
Save Man's deep spirit rising out of Death
Through one vast æon into ethereal forms !
So now in wisdom God selecteth Man
Wedding the healthy mind to limbs of steel."

Again I wondered, and my yearning mind

Expanded swiftly like a tropic flower
Greeting the face of dawn   I saw afar
A flock of flying angels, fanning down
The clouds that hid the sky, 'till, drowned in mist,
The bleeding land lay peaceful as a babe.
Then came a voice from the blue depths of Heaven :—
"Behold," it cried, "the work is well-nigh done,
The Nation's heart is formed and throbs with life,
Against these islands all the world may storm,
And jealous-hearted nations toss their sneers,
But from this day its lightest word shall be
A lesson to the mightiest, kings shall quail
Before its majesty, for they shall know
It lives but to emancipate mankind
From thrall of meanness, misery, and fear."
And as the voice subsided, gentle airs
Blew the white mist away, and left the land
Bare to our eyes.   The stars appeared.   The sun
Poured floods of red, deep down the Western sky.
Then dreamed I that I saw this island fair
Changed to a man, outstretched across the sea ;
Restless he lay, his hand was ever flung
In bold defiance at some daring foe ;
And frowns spread o'er his forehead, like the clouds
That black the brows of mountains ; and his breath
To westward spread like fire that lit the sea ;
And o'er the sea he laid his mighty arm
And stilled it with his will   His heart beat loud,
And I, (made spirit,) saw his bounding blood
Course through his arteries with growing strength !
As thus I dreamed, a spirit touched my soul,
And softly said to me,—"What thinkest thou ?"
Then told I him my dream.   "Ah ! gentle friend,"
Said he, "thy dream is sweet and true ; but late
I came from earth, for I am he men call
The Venerable Bede   The outstretched man
Portrays our country, strong in heart and hand ;

His glowing arteries display Christ's word
Slow coursing through the land   To me the world
Is now but as a toy with which I played
Until I threw it back to quiet Death.
I see the figure of thy dream arise
And stride across the sea to lands afar
I see his head o'ertop the rim of earth
And pierce the twilight like a pillar bold,
A sombre silhouette against the sky.
Rich is his tongue with words,—the words he
    learnt
With eager lips from mine,—and to his voice
Come kindred from afar.   See how they move
'Gainst the blue drapery that falls from heaven,
While with his finger lifted to the skies
He points them to the unseen Throne on high,
A solemn picture looming big with Truth!"

Lured by this vision, long I gazed afar,
Then turned I to the old, sweet soul and smiled —
"Art thou he," asked I, "who taught our English
    tongue
The Testament of John that flowers forth
The mortal passion of our gentle Lord?"
"To that end was I born," he sweetly said.
"Oh! that I more had done my race to raise!
The Present like a mountain-torrent bears
Its falling volume to the floods of Time,
So with the luring Day I lived, and died,
Then fled, as men do all."
                         "Ah," said my Guide .—
"Time hurries onward, stay not with one soul
When all the Universe doth pant for thee;
Around thee are bright eyes and noble hands,
Delightful visions waiting for thine eye.
This sweetened soul would hold thee like a flower
To his charmed self, but there are worlds to see."

"Oh, wondrous Spirit ! " spoke my soul in fear,
"Fain would I linger with this flower of men
And breathe his life's old fragrance evermore ;
Before I vault fresh wonders, let me dream."

Revolt was vain : I felt the speed of Time
Like Bede's resistless torrent bear me on ;
To linger were to die ; so on the stream
Of rushing imagery I was borne.

My Guide and I amid a countless host
Of flying spirits were transported far.
We passed the twilight ; caught the flush of Dawn,
And rushed with glowing speed towards the sun,
Swift as that memorable ray which flew
Out of Sol's burning tresses when the earth
First felt the touch of Light and saw its moon !
Through flying worlds, too small for earth to see,
We sped as fire.   They, like our circling globe,
Full of Creation's joy, spun round the sun
Bent on Life's eager universal quest,
But stayed not our swift flight ;—for spirits pass
Through the dense deeps of Matter light as dew
Drops from the heart of Heaven on Night's dark breast.

E'en though in dreams on earth my mind had strayed
With high imperial Fancy, ne'er had I
Such wonders seen as now lit my new eyes.
Then had my mind strange palaces beheld
With jewelled doors of carven ivory,
And domes made brilliant with earth's rarest gems
Wrought in mosaic by some starry hand
Amid the clouds of Fancy,—mundane all,
Yet ne'er conceived by architect of earth,
For o'er the turrets shone the unknown beams
From the unfathomed Light beyond the Sun,
Seen by no mortal's dainty retina !

Now was I lifted o'er those dreamland scenes,
To such as John on bare, bleak Patmos saw,
And they were real to me.   Real as the day
That smiles on man and tells but half the tale
His mind is born to learn   Real as the sea
That rocks his frail-built body in its arms
And tosses him into the great Beyond ;
Ay, all was real.   The mighty concourse sped,
Just as a river, wandering to the sea,
Fed by the streamlets from the passing hills,
Broadens its way and ploughs the valley deep ;
So spread we o'er th' unbounded realm of space :
For as we floated onward thousands joined
The hurrying, eager multitude of souls,
E'en as the birds at eve will multiply
Coursing through twilight to some goal afar
From cruel eyes of man.   And, as we sped,
I saw strange interminglings of earth's hearts :—
An artizan, who delved the ground for corn,
Was now the compeer of a crownèd King,
Whom Fate had girded with a conquering sword ;
E'en greater was he, for his heart had learned
The sacrifice of Love, which never King
With sad, sword-smitten lands can ever know ;
And I saw women who for Love had died
Treated with greater reverence than a queen,
And fire-tongued patriots by man's passions torn
Seek the sweet presence of those silent hearts
Who know the ways of Heaven   And ah ; alas !
I saw a prelate weeping o'er his days
Ill spent below, cheered by the soothing lips
Of Mary, men call Magdalene in love ,
And he who left his misered gold on earth
Paid homage to the soul of one who felt
The sweet appeal of wistful Poverty.
The murderer sought the murdered and took hands
And touched the angry wounds with healing tears,

The injurer to the injured made sweet love
And sang a new-born melody abroad.
Man's interwoven selfishness had changed;
No longer Might, Place, Beauty, Riches, Power
Prevailed, or Prelate's pardon, or Election's grace,
But only Worth measured by pulse of Love

"Oh! whither journey this vast flight of souls?"
I asked my Guide: "Go they in haste to greet
The fiery-mantled sun that soars afar?"
"Yea," answered he, "these murmuring myriads fly
Responsive to some deep, mysterious law,
As falls a singing streamlet to the vale
From mounts of joy." And, as he ceased, I felt
A sweet-toned voice resounding in my ear;
As though it spoke quite near me, though from far,
And gazing down I saw an angel stand,
Poising his finger to his utterance,
Great with command! "Stay, spirits! stay!" he cried,
"Circle around me, and abide in peace
The coming of the Loved One,—Him who holds
The destinies of all in His wise hand;
He cometh in the chariot of the sun,
Lord of this vast creation; and demands
Mute audience here!" Then with one mighty voice
The concourse cried: "We hear and we obey!"
And round the angel at his potent word
The congregation ranged, tier upon tier,
As from the blue deeps of a restful sea
Rise rocky headlands towering to the sky,
Sculptured in ridges by Time's trembling hand.
Wondering I gazed, for each light astral form
Had melted into each, and I beheld
An untold host of human faces spread
To dizzy heights afar. Then said my Guide:—
"These are the spirits from the grave of Earth,
Gathered as flowrets from the breast of Spring,

Since Adam left his first fair Eden dream,
And, haunted by temptation, planted Earth
With the Forbidden Tree ;—its dainty fruit
Our fateful heritage.   So these sweet souls
Like thee and me have been by trouble torn ;
See how the hand of Saintly Sorrow lines
With Beauty's pencil each ethereal form ,
Far lovelier than yon angel statue-cold,
Who claims command.   But mark ! the Glorious One,
Borne on the blazing orb of gold draws near !"

Then all the vast assembly thrilled with fear,
Such as on earth a listening heart may feel
When, (shrouded with loved Nature's Night-dark green
'Neath the cold gaze of stars,) a spirit voice,
Laden with heavenly language, charms his ear;
So felt this concourse, as the sun stood still,
While th' Almighty breathed his soul abroad :—

" All ye whose pinioned spirits dwelt on earth,
And soared from graves of Sorrow, list to me !
The smallest unit in my Universe
I love, as, on the earth, a mother loves
Her child.   But sad am I for Man   He hears,
But deafness feigneth !   Sees, but gropeth, blind ;
Though my Son's honied lips have taught him Love,
Kissed his blind eyes and thrilled with Truth his ears !
And I, in all my majesty, am grieved
To view earth's continents of ruined Man ;
Yet for the sake of those sweet flowers of Love
That hide with beauty all his brutal stains
The hand of Justice ever I restrain !
I made Man free, his freedom he despoils
With slavery of lust and Death-made fears.
Now hearken, therefore, to my firm decree ,—
If this new nation rise not from the Isles
As flaming torch to light the blinded world,

Then shall the earth be cindered as a coal
In furnace of the sun, so that her face
Shall blotted be from the blue chart of heaven !
What need of Earth if man a brute remain
Like to the ox that, grazing, sleeps, and dies.
Ah ! I am sad for Man, whose heart I made
Free to be noble, that his face might shine
Transfigured by his soul's divinity.
Behold, how he his loveliness has marred !
Let then, this new-born race the Past redeem."

At this a soft remorse spread through the throng,
For all were by earth's imperfections stained,
But when the angel raised his trumpet-voice
In a grand " Hallelujah ".to the Lord,
The myriad concourse in loud chorus joined :—

" Sing we the song that ushered in the Morn
        When Life's great heart was born ;
When Man knelt suppliant to those starry eyes
        That jewel Paradise
When Hope beheld the sun-rise of the Mind
        Scatter the clouds that blind :
When Springlike yearnings lifted Man from Death
        To Heaven's flower-laden breath :
When Great-Hearts fluttered from the breast of Time,
        Eternally sublime :
When Love woke music from the harp that lay
        Forgotten by the way :
When God in mercy flung His wrath afar
        Beyond unmeasured star
        Hail ! Lord of sky and earth !
Baptize with Wisdom Thy new nation's birth !
                        Hallelujah ! "

The chorus ceased, and the great, gold-clad sun
Rolled on its yearly pilgrimage round heaven,

Bearing the God of all.   Him saw we not :
But while He bade the burning sun stand still
The trembling earth afar lost count of hours,
And Man's frail Babels quaked and fell in fear,
As scribes have written in the Book of Time.
And with the throng we fled again to earth
All jubilant with song from grateful hearts,
Proud that the sacred passion in frail man
Should from these Isles arise, a living flame,
True beacon to the empires of the world !

CANTO III

HIGH plained in heaven, fresh visions held our gaze :
Wise, holy men, like flowers, spread through the land :
Deep poets clothed men's thoughts with velvet words,
And gay-clad minstrels roamed thro' town and vale
Singing of valiant deeds and sacred dreams
And stories of sweet piety and love,
So that the people felt romanceful joy,
Crowning the Good with garlands, while the Bad
They draped for ever in a night-steeped veil.
Yet did they bow to Brute-force as their King.

But while we watched upon the war-crushed land
The tender birth of peace, 'twas in high heaven
We saw the wonders shine   The silent moon
Dropped silver o'er the dark green groves of earth
And tipped the dungeon-keep with snow-white lines,
(As tho' it were a fairy phantasy
And not man's dark-browed frowning house of War.)
Hovering, we watched the yellow lamps on earth
Mix with the dropping silver from the skies,
Weird-like, but lovely as a ghostly tale
Told by soft rose-lips blanched with fancied fear.
And suddenly, close by us, flamed a Light

That hid the argent splendour of the moon,
And in the Light the sacred Christ appeared
Crowned with derisive thorns.   I would have flown
To rend the brutal emblem from his brow,
And bathe it from the cauldron of my tears,
But that my Guide forbade me, saying, loud :—
"It is a glory now,—the type to all
Of victory sublime,—and richer far
Than those proud wounds scarred by the steel of war
Upon heroic man.   The Crown of crowns !
Made eloquent of Grief and rich with Love."
So was I silent, and beheld His face,
Starred with the eyes of Sorrow, peering far
Beyond the soul of Man, and yet adorned
With locks like radiant Morn   To Him came one,
Matthew by name, bearing with loving care
An open scroll on which his mortal hand
Had writ the gentle passion of our Lord ,
And lo ! his work was soiled with tender tears,—
For who could watch the frail, loved Christ expire,
Flaming the East with sunlight of His soul,
Without a tearful fancy?   As well bid Heaven
Take back the magic sunshine in a flower,
Or blot the prism from the sunlit tear !
So when St Matthew gazed with aching eyes
Back o'er the solemn pictures of his past,
That he might vision forth our sacred Lord,
The tongue of pity told the troubled tale.
To me 'twere honour wonderful to touch
Our Saviour's magic fingers, but to write
The language of His lips for brother man
Were to be like a sun unto mankind,
Or living incense of the flowers of morn !

With awe I saw a strange majestic cloud,
Blown from the silver regions of the moon,
Form in the heavens a stately snow-white throne

To which our Lord ascended as a King
Great with the might of Virtue and sweet Love ·
And to the thronèd Form St Matthew bowed.
Then from the starry blue came Mark and James
And Luke the healer, and St Peter bold ;—
The heralds of St John, whose mind had dreamed
Of wondrous citadels amid the clouds,
With thrones and angels, lightnings, thunderings,
And universal homage of the Lamb ;
John ! the great bard of Heaven, who paved the way
To high imaginings, and led man's mind
Past all the mortal failures here below
To the great portals of poetic truth,
Where flames the light more rich than bright-eyed
          stars
With his great form came Paul, whose tempest-voice
Had wrecked the temples of the Pagan world,—
Those weak, sand-founded fabrics of Man's thought.
His eyes, like John's, beyond the common ken
Had visions seen unwordable to Man.

These Forms around our Lord's moon-silvered throne,
Each with their scrolls, stood mutely questioning,
Until his gentle voice thus spake to all :—
"Oh ! tender souls ! who have from furrowed earth
Flowered into spirit-forms, I claim thy aid
To ease Man's woes.   Behold ! thy brothers fail
For lack of spirit-food, as dies a flower
Heart-languishing for dew   Man's growing thought
Must build upon the massive stones of Truth
Its citadel to heaven.   I want no creed
To narrow me to Man, no Church to cloud
With veils of fear Man's high-aspiring soul,
No cage to cramp his wings ; for I would fill
His universe with love of Love, with joy
In noble deeds, with scorn of wrong, with Hope
Sun-built upon the mountains ; so that all,

Buddhist or Brahmin, Moslem, Greek, or Jew,
Christian, or heathen may in freedom find
One common temple 'neath this arch of blue,—
The sapphire empire of the throbbing stars
That make the night a wonder and a joy
To eyes that greatly dream. Now bid I thee
Cast on these living Isles thy golden scrolls
Which thine own hands have writ for brother man ;
And I will bid translators great appear
Flushed with the fervour of the Saxon tongue,
So that this new-born race shall know my thought
And learn to love Me whom they have not seen,
'Till in the fullness of the budding years
They shall my mission spread to all mankind ;—
And it shall come to pass that he who looks
In love upon a stone, or flower, or tree,
To woo my Father's secrets, or with eye
And busy brain measures and weighs His stars,
Or in deep delvings of the soul of man
Deciphereth spirit-laws before unseen,
He shall upon the temple-stones of earth
Rise a high priest, walking with holy feet
In the great footsteps of the Deity ! "

He ceased .
And lo ! obedient, each disciple cast
His scroll to earth, and, as they, fluttering, fell,
We saw them multiply, 'till they became
Ten thousand in their flight, and a great wind
Blown from the Mighty Spirit of the skies
Scattered them far, 'till even the woods had tongues,
The mountains dreamed, the valleys rose and sang
In sympathy with man, and rivers rolled
Tumultuous music to the impatient sea,
Leaping in splendour round the laughing land.

Blown by the singing wind the silver throne

Hurried towards the Morn, whose ruddy eye
Smiled on the gladdened Isles ; then to the earth
My wondering soul was borne by my kind Guide,
And I beheld the historic march of kings
Fended by Saxon spears, foiled in the fight
By the usurping Danes, with milder rule ;
And ever to our sickening eyes there rose
Lean, wild, insurgent fingers steeped in blood
Clutching in envy at each kingly crown,
From Alfred to the giant Conqueror.
Each king was bandied like an idle ball
'Tween Life and Death,—a humour of a day,
A storm-clad day, lit by no sun of Love.
To name the wild succession would but fill
A page of weariness   But busy Rome,—
Wise, dull, material, scheming, selfish Rome,
Blind to the light that lured St Peter's eyes,—
Sent forth her prelates to the rising realm
To sap the growing splendour of the King,
And bind his crown around her Papal brow
But all in vain ; in that grand cavalcade
A wonderous Spirit-Form all fearless rode
Upon a prancing and high-mettled steed ;
With her strong hand she bent the People's bow,
Lifted their sword, and shook their deadly spear,
Hurled their wild battle-axe and thundered loud
At frowning castles, full of dungeon fears ,
She sought the Light, and filled the heart of Man
With mountain-Hope, and gazed with prophet-eye
Through gathering centuries of cloudy shame
To where the sun flamed on the ripening corn.
My guide then said to my enquiring eyes .—
" Freedom is her great name whose heart beats slow
In priest-craft's realm of superstitious fear,
But in Man's mystic temple of the soul
She kneels before the universal God
And sings for aye her golden litany

With lips of fire, unlocks the shackles forged
By hard hearts for a brother, and decrees
That neither king, nor priest, nor Pontiff proud
Shall stand between Man's conscience and his God.
To her thy race have aye proud dalliance paid,
And to her frown thy kings have bowed in fear.
Yea, all the earthly armaments of Rome
Have dashed in impotence 'gainst her free heart,
As a vain bee batters a soaring mountain."
                        I rejoiced
To see her lead this proud, fierce, crownèd throng,
Like happy captives in her lily hands ;
Kings that were symbols of a people's joy,
Not grinding tyrants typical of fear.
E'en as he spake I heard the Spirit-form
Break into magic song that charmed our ears :—

FREEDOM'S SONG

1.

When the heart of man gazes with joy to heaven's
      eyes
    And breathes the proud breath of the free,
When the flash of Truth flames thro' the stubble of
      lies
    Oh ! then comes great gladness to me.

2.

When I lead a King captive to thoughts that are
      born
    From a spirit as free as the wave,
And I see his eyes pity the frail and forlorn
    Oh ! then I rejoice in a slave !

3

But when I behold him walk thro' the wide land
    As free as a bird on the wing,
And he for the soul of the people doth stand
    Oh ! then I rejoice in a King !

4

And to England's green isles in the blue of the sea,
    Enriched with a tribute of foam,
I am mystical mistress and ever will be
    Beneficent queen of her home

5

Oh ! lift up your heads, ye down-trodden, afar,
    The babe that ye nurse on your knee
Shall rise with the centuries, shine like a star,
    And throb with the heart of the free !

6

Till Earth all light-hearted shall lift its wide wings,
    And through the wide ether shall fly,
To bear to the Maker of all happy things
    The happiest home in the sky.

And as she ceased her singing, lo ! she came
Unto my Guide and me, with heaving breast,
And pulses all on fire, and to our eyes
Revealed huge bastions built by brutal man
Against his brother, cities fenced with fear ;
Men mail-clad 'gainst their kindred ; Convents, cells,
And monasteries, filled with moody minds,
Who scorned fair Nature and the Tempter dared
'Neath th' eternal mockery of the stars !
Yet when she came where Love lived in sweet dreams
She passed away in silence, as though earth
No longer needed her to break with force
Man's citadel of woe

CANTO IV

So wondered I.   My soul seemed helpless borne
Upon the passion of a human sea
Leaping beyond the bastions of control,
And when my Guide, glowing with prophet-words,
Praised this brute nation to my angry ears,
I felt as feels a doubting tropic eye
When shown sweet pictures of an English May,—
Fairy-strewn meadows buttercupped with gold,—
For round me lay a human wilderness,
And to my Guide I ventured chiding words :—
" Behold ! these men of storm are cultureless ;
The sword clangs down on guilt and innocence,
And woman lives in morbid fear of man ;
The child is taught to view nobility
In coat-of-mail, and casque, and vaunting plumes,
In sword and cross-bow, battle-axe and spear,
Emblems of enmity 'tween brother man,
And slowly flowers in him the look of love ! "
Once more my Guide, with my impatience vexed,
Soared with me into heaven and showed me worlds
(Flung untold ages back from breeding suns
To cool in space,) still warm with smouldering fire,
And all unfit for holy Nature's dreams
Of seeds and plants, and tender flesh like Man's.
" Wait, wait," said he, " as these hot worlds must wait
For their perfection ! Look thou, too, within
At thine own heart, and tell me if thy years
Have marshalled thee to victory ? Dost thou not
Still worship winsome eyes and thrill with joy
When fair temptations trip into thy ken ?
Yet, since these days, eight centuries have borne
Their brows of Wisdom to thy garnering mind ! "

Then like a thunder-roll his anger died

And all was still , so still that I was awed
With the great quiet round my stifled soul.
But, as on earth, in storm-time, sullen calm
Seems the mute herald of the demon wind,
So now in the dull distance I could hear
Mutterings of wrath, howlings as of a gale
Among the granite mountains, and there came
A black-draped cloud, sudden as strides the sun
Into the tropic morn.   My heart leapt fast
In fear as round us crept the vapourous veil.
Lurid it was with sprites whose teeming tongues
Had once bred lies into the ears of earth,
And now, in haste, they passed us raving by ;—
Raving, not at the Universe or God
But at themselves for having dared to be
Didactic on the earth with blinded minds !
Their new eternity o'erwhelmed with woe
To feel that they had turned the hands of Time
Back in Man's centuries, in face of God !
For they had wrought theologies and hells,
Had walked not with stern Science thro' the spheres,
Or peered into the crucible of Earth,
But had distorted God to baby-Man !
With great Augustine they had imaged God
Outside His Universe , His giant skill
Controlling, quenching, pruning here and there
With fusing Thought, as we with finite minds
Gaze searchingly through microscopic lens
At wonders infinite.   But, feeling now
The pulsing heart of God through earth and stars,
Through Man and secret spirits of the deep,
They strive to sweep delusion from Man's eyes.
Great tears were in that cloud and sorrow sore.
And as I gazed upon my kindly Guide
A tender pathos swum into his eyes ·—
" Ah ! stricken souls," cried he, " whose tongues long
          dead,

Still clarion falsehood to the ears of men,
Would I could blow thy thoughts like dust afar
Or lock them deep in dim Oblivion's grave;
But thy false words must linger till they fade
Like fleeting violet in the bleeching sun."

It was to me a wonder to behold
That weeping cloud full of repentant tears.
I wept with joy.   It seemed as though wise hands
Were stretched from heaven to quench the treacherous
    lights
Left on the earth to lure unwary minds.
Mohammed wept with Buddha and the shams
Who walked in surplices in Christ's great name,
Dead to his laws though frolic with his tongue,
Were stricken sore with fear.   I saw full well
That all the false philosophies of man
Were but as blighted blossoms on a tree
Dedicate to decay.   There was no God
Who fondled Falsehood near His sacred throne.

With flattering face I turned to my kind Guide
And thanked with eloquent looks his pictures rare
Until his mind thawed 'neath the sun of Love
And flowed in liquid language round my soul.
He conjured to my gaze my Norman sires
Bred in the lap of France, rhyming their tongues
To the red, luring lips of Gallic maids,
Whose tender sweet, seductive eloquence
Soon drowned their Saxon in the foreign flood
Of liquid Latin that o'erwhelmed the world.

Then saw I Norman William's giant form
Rise in hot anger and with lips of France
Swear to break down the English Harold's realm.
Then o'er the sobbing sea the Norman host
Bore their hot hearts unto the Sussex shore,

And spread their valourous army to the siege
Of Harold's England, rent with feud and fear.

So Culture came with clarion and with axe
And all the brutal ceremony of war,
Armed with the tender tongue of Normandy
To win our winsome Isles,
But the sweet tongue suited no Saxon lip ;
It fell on English ears as brilliant dew
Jewels the blossoms of a golden morn,
And not as torrents sweeping from the hills
The utterance of years.   But still it lit
With lightness every witful phrase and touched
With delicacy lips of Saxon song

I saw in Culture's train Beauty-taught minds,
Clad in the craftsman's garb, with dreamy gaze
Grave Gothic architects with Southern eyes
Made the land fair with monuments in stone ;
Through oriel windows rich with pictured lore
I saw the awakened eyelids of the Morn
Greet me ; and the soft moon peeped like Love's dream
Through interlacing arches, quaintly carved
With saints and angels, whose outspreading wings
Seemed ripe to fan the fairy fane to heaven
To install it 'mid the enchantment of the stars.
From stern, black castles frowned the Norman power
Fearing though feared, feudal and unforgiving ;
Yet in the armoury the artist wrought
Poetic fancies on the murdering sword ;
The artist in the workshop taught the tools
New magic of design.   Upon the walls
The hands of ladies tapestried their dreams
Of mural ornament ; monks in their cells
Delved out the wealth of Greek and Roman lore ;
Fair women courtesied to their loving lords
In dainty raiment wrought with artist-pains ;

Politeness and Sweet Culture, hand in hand,
Roamed through the streets, as silent monitors
Chiding unruly minds   It was as though
A breath of Summer thawed the Wintry land
And lured the landscape to put on its flowers;
As though a maid unconscious of her grace
First in a silver mirror read her eyes.

My Guide in rapid movement turned the years,
And I beheld Imagination sweep
With flaming wings over the waking Isles.
With new-born vision poets wove the earth
And all the wondrous galaxy of worlds
Into the stage of Life; and pictured God
Throned on his thousand suns uplifting Christ
To sacrificial slaughter for Mankind.
A savagely grand vision; fanning high
The Spartan flame then smouldering in our sires.
It wrought perpetual wonder.   I beheld
The sturdy Saxon strive to walk like Christ
To His proud goal, blind Justice by His side.
Though stormed by Statecraft, Priestcraft, Wealth, and
    Power,
Soul after soul went to the sacrifice,
A victim to the charms of cruel Truth
Like their loved Lord!   Crusaders sought the Grail
And the great Lord's applause in the wild wish
To fend the Holy Land from impious hands;
As tho' each corner of the flower-clad world
Were not His habitation and His joy;
As tho' a place were sacred to a soul!
But so it was and so, alas! it is,
With mystic eyes we see ghost-haunted tombs,
Tho' the flowered soul smiles 'neath unsullied suns
And dallying daisies laugh above his bones!
Freedom was with us, and for her and Truth
Men greatly dared, marching with iron tread

'Gainst tyrant insolence in places proud,
And near the hem of Christ, flung Self to death !

But from the turmoil rose the emotioned song ;
And how shall I describe the sacred sounds
That greeted my rapt ears as my kind Guide
Led me to where the anthems of our race
Were safely stored !   The fabric hung like threads
Of gossamer spun from a golden sun,
A vast suspended palace on whose walls
In lovely lines our Isles were tapestried,
Web-woven maps of fairy colours formed
A place of charm, a spirit-place, God-made,
The garner-house of our enchanted song ;
Not a dull hall of Matter, for it hung
Suspended from the sun 'gainst all the laws
Of Giant Gravitation, whose large arms
Safe poise the sailing worlds in heaven's blue sea.
Fit fabric for such furnace-working minds
Which can within the crucible of thought
Melt the great globe into a lens of glass
And thro' it gaze into the Great Beyond,
Such magnitude surrounds the mortal mind !
It can the mountains flame, the valleys fill
With wonder ; and at a touch transform
The meanest to the mightiest.
It was far lovelier than a home of stones
Made rich with gold and silver , more like dreams
That tend upon the dying of the sun
Upon a summer evening, when the West
Builds in a moment a vast dome of Art
With colours mingled by translucent hands,
Watched by one brightening star.   There at their ease
Sat our enchanted singers ; souls who breathed
Their breath in song, as a loved bird inspired
Trembles his passion to the sinking sun
Amid empurpled branches.   Tier upon tier

They sat ; and great my joy, when, to my Guide,
Silver-tongued Chaucer rose with deep salute
And to him said :—

               "O ! spirit of our race !
Ye made me earliest minstrel of thy tongue.
I took the flowers and wove them in my song
Until thy tongue became to me like flowers.
I culled the blossoms from afar and near
And ranged them with sweet Fancy, and I breathed
The breath of Life upon them, and they joyed
To breathe my music back again to me.
My country's lips grew dulcet with sweet sounds
Or rose in passion like a furnace-flame
That leaps towards the sun, Apollo-like,
Imparting rapid fire from soul to soul.
I taught the orator to draw the tear
And then to laugh the tender pearl away ;
To woo , to scorn ; to fire, then damp the flame ;
To move the multitude with gusty breath
As bows the forest to the wailing wind ;
Or to control them with the sweet word—' Peace,'
As quiet sunshine quelleth the proud storm.
And as I wove the language to my tongue
I felt as though the ages yet unborn
Came round me with new lips and vocal eyes
To bless me ,
And in a dream I saw the Babel world
Fall down in adoration to my words,
Which I had dowered with all harmonies
Of mortal chords ; all passion of sweet love
Culled from the dead lips of the centuries.
And all men learnt my language and grew bold
To call me brother, 'till my race's thought
Passed swiftly round the world from lip to lip
And nations knew each other and took hands.
Then Babel ended and the world grew young
Oft since have I the gates of earth unclosed

And filled the breath of the enraptured Morn
With spirit-odours blown from lips of heaven.
And lo! my lovely English like the trailing rose
Doth talk sweet Liberty to all the lands!"

Great was my joy at these enkindling words,
But greater still to know he lived and loved
Whom weeping eyes had seen devoutly laid
In his proud Abbey tomb in the dusk years.
I felt the Past was with me, and my Guide
Smiled at my innocent, delighted eyes,
'Till a commotion moved the assembled forms
As Shakespeare rose, rich with his wisdom-tongue,
To greet my Guide ; then fell a listening silence
On expectant ears —
            "Hail! Great Spirit! Hail!"
The poet cried, "Ye sunned me into flower,
And as a flower I turn toward my sun.
When I amid thy meadow-daffodils,
And cowslips, and empurpled thyme was born,
I learnt the song of Nature, as the birds
Learn music from the spirits in the trees ;
But in the town the Book of Man I read
And said to him the litany of his soul
I was the priest-translator of his moods,
Weaving his proverbs into holy verse,
Music divining in the sound of words
And now I live in this great hive of minds,
In this stored sweetness of our poet-flowers,
To yield my honey to my race unborn
What care I for the wonders of the stars
While brother man lets terror steal his soul,
And hurls himself in ignorance 'gainst rocks
While sailing in the storms of mortal seas.
My race! my race! Man's hope lives in my race!
To me eternity is but a day
And I can wait as God waits at Man's heart,

For spirits know not Man's small count of hours.
So with a patience infinite I lure
My country's mind to true nobility.
Each year I watch the Volumes of its Thought
Like great ships launched upon the sea of Time ;
Some sink to Death unbuoyant as a stone,
While the choice few, floating with magic ease,
Sail in full glory to the gates of Fame,
Blown by the breath of Praise.   Their pilot I ;
For on the true work of the noble mind
We spirits ever tend when giant Thought
Springs from the heart of Man.   I see afar
Th' unfolding future of my country's power,—
The power that welds all nations into one,—
And lo ! men cry, ' Behold, we work for Good !'
And sacrifice and pity are unknown,
For Christ's great sermon on the immortal Mount
Becomes the decalogue of all Mankind.
Let mighty God give wings to that fair day.
When great Copernicus flung Earth to space
And fixed the sun before Man's wondering eyes
Each heart took fear to see Man's ancient dreams
Lost in Infinitude ; but when our race
Raised Darwin from the dust of science-thought,
Lo ! we saw God evolving from the Past
Man's mystic soul ; raising for him the flowers,
The fruits, the trees, and the year's corn ; for him
The sun, the moon, earth and the million stars ;
And Man's great sight of Matter shrunk to naught
Beside the vast unfoldings of his soul.
Then, Spirit of my Race ! with thy vast Voice
Put heart into Mankind, 'til hate, and scorn,
And frenzy of possession shall become
As a dead vulture to the soul of Man,
That all may live for all.   To this great end
New poets dream, sounding abroad their song,
So to this end we pour our influence down

As sunlight on the land."
                        Great the applause
Of this effusive throng at this grand dream,
And great my joy to hear!   The Universe
Seemed small to me as a toy-acorn held
In a child's hand : my soaring mind and all
My brother-minds but played with it, e'en as
The simple child plays with its acorn-toy.
Fast-founded Thought, though by our Science scorned
May prove a firmer fabric than a weighed
And measured star, and may through ages grow
Into divinity, even as God
Is greater than His star and simple I
Greater than my vain lines   And I was proud
To feel that the eternal heat of Life
Was on my people poured and that to all
Who spoke my language came the constant call
To sing the song of the Almighty Voice
To all the listening lands.   Glory to come ;
Glory to kindle in the humblest heart
The flame to light Man to the eternal paths
Of Love and Joy.
                        Thus, dreaming, I beheld,
(As my great Guide bore me towards our world,)
The magic poet-palace in the heavens
Fade as a flower away, and I was left
With Nature and her stars, watching the round
And palpitating earth chasing its dream
In circles round the sun.   But, hurrying forth,
As 'twere from solid earth, came a fair form
That halted in our way.   His eyes were lit
With brightness as of noon when flowers exhale
Their kisses to the sun and the Day's eye
Laughs Sorrow far away.   His limbs were draped
With garments such as Morn flings on the breast
Of the sun, when, from his swoon of sleep,
Apollo rises bathed in floods of dew

And, as I gazed, wondering as at a dream,
I saw above his forehead, flamed in gold,
His name, " Prosperity." Drawn by the sight
I flew to him, forgetful of my Guide,
And to him said :—"Art thou my Country's friend
Or enemy ? " And he, calm as a glass
That silently reflects a face of storm,
Said :—" Friend am I, if I be truly known ;
But if she bid another reap her corn,
Or hire a hand to helm her argosies
Across the foam and pay them with dead gold,
Whilst she in idleness doth flirt with Time,
Then am I not her friend, but a kind curse
Boonless and unproductive as a dream :
For gold is but the gilt of my fair name.
When truly known I will her prince of friends
And guardian of her princes be, for I
Will bless the work-proud hand and wisdom-brow
With fruit of high attainment, and will be
The power, the joy, and dignity of toil
If I be truly hers she will not let
The palsied beggar eye her opulence
With sad-eyed scorn, but from unmisered wealth
Will fill the hungry crannies of the land.
If I be truly hers and she be mine
She will entice the world to live in peace,
Guarding the rights of all with clarion breath
That shall affright the Wrong and wake to life
The dying Right. If she be truly mine
From the impassioned artist she will woo
The magic of his mind, and, as his slave,
Build up the mystic mansion of his Fame
Till it become the reverence of all eyes,
And she shall be twice reverenced in him
Who came to her as comes a thought from God ! "

With this he ceased. His words were strange to me ;

D

For I had looked on Poverty as dew
Sent from refreshing heaven to lift mankind
As flowers from sordid, earthly, fainting dreams :
Yet were the words full wise, and as my Guide
And I gazed in his face, behold, he burst
Into a rhyming melody of words —

PROSPERITY'S SONG

"I am Man's passion
  From cradle to grave,
See how I fashion
  Him into a slave !
Hear how he cries to me
'Send me Prosperity,'
Be he a noble or be he a knave !

"See how he measures
  In silver and gold
All of Life's treasures
  As dross that is sold !
Yet he who cries to me
'Send me Prosperity,'
Knows not the glory I have to unfold.

"But in this nation
  My skill shall unite
In magic creation
  Goodness with Might !
So when she cries to me
'Send me Prosperity,'
I slowly peep forth as she toils for the Light !"

And with these words he fled.   Faint felt my heart
With these resplendent visions crowding fast
Into the wide arena of my brain ;
Yet quickly as it came the faintness fled
Flushed with divining Thought, and I was borne
From sight to sight as bees from flower to flower.

CANTO V

YE who have seen o'er shoreless seas of Thought
The magic, serried, restless-hearted waves
Break into flowers of silver-fretted foam
'Neath realms of fairy Fancy; or have felt
Imagination's glorious tide sweep on
In wonder past the helmless hulls that lie
Wingless of glory, in the soul-stirred sea,
While million stars of Hope and suns of Joy
Beckon the buoyant soul for ever on :
Ye who have felt thus know how hard my task
To find fit words to grace Thought's argosy;
For Thought, born boundless, by no words is bound.
Yet must I write my Dream ere palsy claim
The silence of my hand; so on and on
My pen must weep its letters to the page.

Vision came fast on vision. I had seen
The germinating spirit-flow of Thought
Pass through dead millions into my great race;
I had seen Christ upon his silver throne
Cast his scrolled gospel on our yearning Isles;
And I with spirit-multitudes had flown
To hear th' Almighty's voice with high command
Break from the golden chamber of the sun;
I had seen Culture in the arms of War,
And Freedom masking in a coat-of-mail;
I, too, had learnt that every trivial act
Played on our theatre of life was stored
In unseen archives by some unseen hand,
Like photographs on fairy films of sky;
And I had learnt that Thought flew past like light
From man to man, and star to star, safe bound
In the eternal arteries of God;
And now my Guide bade me, in joy, behold

The historic page, beckoning an angel-form
Unto my side, above whose brow I read
In signs of gold, her name, " Recordia ;"
For she was the fair keeper of a book
Wherein were stored the annals of our race,—
A costly volume in " The Book of Time."
A wondrous book it was with leaves of fire
Whereon was miniatured my country's deeds.
Each leaf of fire teemed with our magic life,
And words were uttered by the tiny forms
That leapt to action in the flaming page.
And as each leaf died down another rose
To tell its fairy picture to my brain ;
And when the book was closed lo ! the bright leaves
Re-formed again to tell their pictured tales
To others yearning with historic eyes.
It was as though a mind o'erwrought with dreams
Might see a vista of eternity
Flash through his brain ; e'en as a man may read
The memory of his life without the aid
Of slowly creeping words.   Quick flew the scenes.
King after King passed by me in despair,
Queen after Queen rose up and kissed their lips
Shedding sad tears ; and when I asked my guide
Why these in sad procession wandered by,
He said :—" These are thy kings who knew not love
But rose with arms of power to grip the land
In close embrace, forgetful of the claims
Of the vast, thinking multitude, whose eyes
Looked up to them as to new gods from heaven,
And looked in vain !"
I saw bluff Harry blaze upon his crown
" Head of the Church," crushing with cruel hand
The Church he ruled, and in his train six queens
Trod Eve's green earth in fear.   I saw him write
With nimble wit unto the Pope of Rome,
And as he wrote he laughed his soul to tears.

And I saw Papal garments rent with rage
As the small letter lit the Papal eyes
With unforgiving Light from our proud realm.
Up surged a thousand foes, like a wild sea,
With burnished breast-plates, bows, and flashing
    spears,
And at their head rode the great Pope of Rome
Breathing anathemas In his rich train
Crept gaudy-coloured prelates, short of breath
With immemorial cursings, bearing high
Gibbets and thumbscrews, faggots, fire, and Death's
Fell instruments of torture, 'till, alas !
The world rolled round in fear.   And then I heard
False lips chant praise to Christ in whose loved
    name
They dared to torture tongues to win a lie.
Fear's icy fingers crept along my frame
As the vain blasphemy profaned my ears,
And when I saw a shadow blind the sun
I hid my eyes, for well my instinct knew
It was the angry breath of the Unseen
Passing 'tween heaven and earth.   Yet the great God
Cursed not the mountain or the vale, but lit
The world with flush of light each morn !   On came
The foes against my race o'er land and sea
Until I saw a queen with ivory hand
Dole out the niggard gold to fend our shores.
Around her flocked strong men with eyes a-glow
With warm humanity, men who saw God
Imaged in tender flowers, through whom a light
Shone as from heaven, waking the world entombed
In the necropolis of Custom ; Men
Who held Truth, God, and God, Truth ! Men who
    dared
All for the glowing light that lit their souls !
These saw I round the Elizabethan Queen
Who bade them arm their fingers for the fight.

Then saw I barks shoot from our jagged shores
Laden with Glory waiting to be born,
As from the West Spain's gaudy galleons came
Armed with the wrath of Rome to lay us low.
But in the sky, behold! wise spirits flew
Fanning commotion, and the storm grew black
In the eye of heaven, and the waters wrathful boiled
'Till the leviathan had scant time to catch
His meed of breath, and the proud galleons strove
In fury vain against Omnipotence
I saw our island skippers buzz like bees
Around the Spanish boats to sting their sides.
Then heard I cries of terror on the main
As death engulfed them, and a pæan rang
In thunder through the clouds. (Wrath reigned in
    Rome
And sad eyes wept in Spain desolate tears.)
Then came mute exodus of girdled priests
From our tired land teazed with Theology.

All this I saw in the leaping leaves of flame
With growing wonder, and to my Guide I cried ;—
" Behold! great glory to my race is born
And now I joy! Rich with illumined mind
Each heart beats true to Principle and Truth
And fights as one against a world of foes
In scorn of gain! Why came these foes from far
With stir of war? Why did Rome's hierarchy
Spit from their tongues hot hate at my loved land?
As well might they employ their guilty hands
To weave a coverlet around the sun
As with vain thought to dare to quench the Light
That flashes visions through the soul of Man!
Galileo's voice defies the Papal rage
Of long ago, and still our Jesus flowers
Upon his cruel tree, and Socrates
From his dull hemlock draught rises as an

Immortal, and with 'impious' breath still chants
The bridal-song of unborn centuries!
O cloud-wrapt giants that in anger rose
And from the firmament smote Olympian fire,
And ye wild waves that dashed with foam of light
'Gainst the dark hulls of Rome, I gaze on ye
With the stored eyes of all the centuries,
And hid behind thy trembling wrath I see
The magic of God's hand, touching with fire
Thy black-hued batteries and setting free
The vast Imagination of my race
From the set folds of priestly draperies!"

At this my Guide smiled with approving eyes
And bade uprise again the flaming leaves.
All the Elizabethan glory passed
Like sunrise o'er my soul as I beheld
The wisdom-spirits from artistic Greece
With the ripe grace of old mingle and dream
With my new race, while Hebrew prophets brought
Celestial language to entrance their ears :
The sweet divinity of happiest words
Adorning happiest thought.   And then I gazed
On Drake and all his heroes of the flood
Wrestling with Death for high nobility,
My muscles straining at their daring deeds.
And I was proud to see my country bear
Fair Freedom on her shoulders as a cross
Up Calvaries of trouble, not to death,
But to her peerless place, whence she controls
The labyrinthian issues of the world.
'Twas Freedom's patience taught my toiling race
The magic virtue of the people's will,
The gathered good of all, the common voice
That never framed a dissolute decree.
Within the leaping flames, as the years fled,
I heard great Hampden use the people's breath

With Eliot and Pym, while Charles, the king,
Heeding no people, walked in scorn with Death
To a regretful glory, martyred quite
By Folly's favourite, Pride   I saw the storm
That scourged our Isles tossing the hearts of
    men
In Passion's gale.   And through the storm I heard
The Hebrew songs upon our alien lips,
'Till we became a wonder in the world,
A people pulsing with the love of Truth !
(The love that sings the Psalm of Righteousness
To each created ear, until, in joy
Music-enchanted footsteps reach the peak
Of vastest vision in the observatory
Of Earth !) O ! I could sing of dreams that charmed
Our race in those wild days ; dreams that have
    yet
To dawn upon the night of half mankind,
But 'tis enough to tell how English hearts
With careful toil built the great fane of fanes
Where dwells primeval Justice, who of old
By demons of Authority was torn
And bruised, but who, by Freedom fended now,
Triumphant reigns over the monarch-world

Full weary grew I of the flaming leaves
Until great Cromwell with his gaze on heaven
Leapt into life.   Then saw I kingdoms move
In jealous fear as he forbore to wear
The type of Sovereignty, but stood, soul-white
Before his fellows as he faced his God,—
(The Being babbled of by baby-lips
Of Man,—for not a river of fine tears
Could cleanse bold Cromwell's murder stains
From our more modern hands.   He only knew
The Jew's Jehovah brutal as a bull
By priestly council reared, and yet our Christ

Had lived and wept and died to show in love
A father and the brotherhood of all)

Weeping I sighed and wondered , and my Guide
Bade fair Recordia close the magic book
That I might gaze on other wonders round,
More hopeful and more beautiful and free

So I was borne by my great Guide afar
Into a magic hall of Paradise
Where stood a concourse of my Nation's peers,—
Peers not of blood but of distinction born,
The hall was built, not as we build on earth
By measured rule and architectural line,
But blazing planets in small orbits moved
Around a central star, and from their sides
Poured feathery streams of light, which, mingling,
    formed
Strange, moving walls into a palace-dome
That sparkled with a hundred varying tints
Of ruby, violet, emerald, cream and gold.
The central-sun,—the lode-star—was aglow
With bright, outspreading, many-coloured rings
Like those we see round Saturn's fairy form
When thro' the crystals of the earth we gaze
With Newton's learned eyes   Upon these rings
The concourse stood, while on the star itself
The orator upon a peak would stand
And flower forth the poetry of all.
It was a lovely scene, though magical,
A complicated, strange, artistic whole.
Sights as enchanting few on earth may see
Unless, perchance, upon a summer day
We catch the poppies fluttering 'mid the corn,
A blaze of scarlet dashed on green and gold ,
Or in a lordly dome our eyes may steal

Remembrances, by kindly favour shown,
Of pictured landscapes lit by Turner's eyes !

And as I gazed, lo ! with unbounded joy
I saw great Cromwell with the murdered Charles
Move hand in hand, honouring the eyes of all.
" Nay," said my heart, " Heaven has not surely made
These two opposing souls familiar friends
While we grow great in warring o'er their bones ! "
But so it was, for the too-kingly Charles
Up to the mountain-tribune led his foe
Who flooded all his listeners with his tears :—

" Alas ! " said he, " I stand before you all
A second Cain, whose English hand is dyed
With eloquent blood.   I could have stemmed the
        storm ;
I could have cowed my warrior's hearts, but then
My England would have ambled as of old
Through the worn paths of history ; but I
Heard Liberty in every heart complain
Of its mute thraldom to a single king
Who could be but a man,—a selfish man,—
Not the large conscience of a people fraught
With hope for all the living world ; so I
Fanned the great storm, used it to winnow Truth
For my great Nation's heart, and now I stand
With sorrow in my soul for all this war,
And yet with joy to know our martyred Charles
Joins with us all to wish our country well.
The storm has passed whose tempest-breathings blew
The *Mayflower's* argosy across the foam
To plant the heart of Britain in the West,
But I and Charles and all his kindred kings
Stand here as Captains of a buoyant ship
To help its progress through the wondering world.
I taught my country's hand the art of war,

I laid the scourge of Blake upon the seas,
I fostered commerce, tore the castles down,
For lo ! ten thousand warriors to my side
Had sprung to life for righteousness and love
Of Liberty.   And now no hand may stay
My country's course.   King after king would fall
Who dared to over-ride the people's will.
Their majesty would fade as doth a cloud
From sovereign gold to a dull, humble gray
In the sunk furnace of the sun !
No right had I to quench the breath of kings ;
No right had they to bind fair Liberty ;
So I and my rough soldiers in God's name
Loosed Liberty's bonds, and she in frenzy drew
Her trembling sword upon a breathing king.
Despise me not for my most murderous hand
O, ye assembled nobles of the realm !
I weep, myself, for my iniquity ;
For now I see my life with my cleansed eyes
And all remorseful——"
                        But at these words the king
Cut with the diamond current of his tears
Stepped forth with regal gesture and began :—

" Peers of my country ! let us dry his tears.
His words are arrows in my guilty breast ;
'Twas I, not he, who held my kingdom down,
'Twas I, who, like a rude assassin, stood
Threatening my country's throat, to beg an alms
To pamper this royal pauper of the realm ;
And, without Cromwell, she had never walked
Two centuries in the forefront of the world.
My head was forfeit for my daring deeds,
He came and wisely moved me from the scene
For I was stubborn as a British bull.
But when I rose into the realm of heaven
And when he followed with his duty done,

And all his warriors (who had scattered far
The chivalry of my Rupert of the Rhine,)
Melted again into the people, lo !
Like a fair river yearning for the sea
Amid o'erhanging roses and through meads
Of boundless fancy, my great country flowed.
Applaud him ! bless him ! wipe away his tears ! "

Then circling Cromwell with a loving arm
He led him from the tribune, while the crowd
In loud approval signified their joy :
And, as in union they descended, I
Beheld another slowly wend his way
To the vacated forum.   He had eyes
That gazed afar, peopling the vacant air
With vast imaginings.   For a brief space
I knew him not, 'till memory's eyes prevailed
And brought the great-brained Milton to my view,
Pained with his vast conception of Despair ;
Whose mind, alas ! had dulled the earth with gloom,
Unlike a flower, a rainbow, or a star
That every moment on the inner eye
Imprints its dream of beauty.   His raised hand
To instant hush awed the great multitude,
And I felt filled with fear as he began .—

" Peers of my Country ! hear with open mind !
Lo ! I am he who on my century wrote
A doleful dream, daring to picture God
Gazing with just but ever cruel eyes
At his own Universe and fallen Man.
Each drop of ink that sparkled on my pen
Mirrored the conscience of the Puritan.
Better, indeed, had I defamed a rose,
Painted with infamy a maiden's cheek,
Or blacked the blue of heaven, than to have dared
With chosen words to measure out the Mind

Of Him who made the rose and lit the stars.
How ye must scorn me ! ye who now behold
His Presence with your wide, unsullied eyes !
Would that some soul on earth might prune my work
Of its proud heresies and leave untouched
The bloom of poesy upon its page.
But 'twould be all in vain   In every line
Man's vanity has crept as creeps a worm
Into the secret folios of the rose.
When Priest Colenzo ushered in the light
Of sacred thought upon the early Word
The mind of Man was dazed : then how much more
May scorning thought wither my sacred prose.
Alas ! for ingenuity of words,
For Man's dull look into his own warm heart !
A baby's thought that sees God in a star
Transcends the small conceit of him who dares,
Lost in the luxury of a scholar-mind.
Mould God to his vanity as though He
Who snows the mountains, flowers the dreaming vales,
Could ever be designed by Man's dull mind,
Better be heathen Greek or Roman born
And dream of God hid in a beauteous form
Than dare to analyze the Magic Mind,
Who made in love the riddle of the rose
And my warm soul !   But I did more, far more ,
'Twas I who wrote ' Murder's Apology !'
And whitewashed Cromwell from the death of Charles,
Hurrying my note with pleadings eloquent
Through all the states of Earth, who shook their heads
At my vain words   As though a poet-mind
Could cut a brother down and feel no fear !
Bitterly rues my heart its cruel joy.
I should with all my brother poets live
In love within the Palace of the Sun
But for these thoughts of blood that stain my soul
And bid me in this Hall of Spirit-Peers

Attend to guide my country with my voice
To higher, holier altitudes of thought."

I saw stern Cromwell and the lavish Charles
Move to the poet at these anxious cries ;
And with soft words and gentle argument
They eased his tempest-mind until his lips
Touched with his fiery spirit burst in song —

> " In the glowing light of Truth,
>   Fearing not the storm,
>   Greatly daring,
>   Nobly caring,
>   Anglo-Saxons form !

> " Form a living line of Light
>   That the false betrays,
>   Marching gaily,
>   Singing daily,
>   Love's perpetual praise !

> " 'Till the holy Light shall spread
>   With a magic speed,
>   Making nations
>   New creations,
>   Love their only creed.

> " Tho' thy phalanx pierce the False
>   With thy spears of Light,
>   'Mid the crying
>   Of the dying
>   Shadows of the Night,

> " Yet the world shall wake to peace
>   With a new-born face,
>   Finding glory
>   In the story
>   Of the Saxon race ! "

With this he ceased and my great Guide knelt down
In courtesy to his magnetic mind;
And all his brother-spirits likewise fell
Prone on their knees thrilled with his throbbing song.
Thus had I seen in one wild glowing hour
How enemies of sovereign might on earth
Become in spirit-realms eternal friends.
So, too, I saw, with an unmeasured joy,
How every senator of my great land
Became a mightier senator in heaven,
And strove with magic influence to mould
The thoughts that flood the living race below,
And, turning to my Guide, I thanked him well
For all this light new shed upon my mind.

CANTO VI

So strode we o'er the dust of centuries,
My heightened mind alert, tho' full of fear,
At all the unfolding wonders. Vainly sought
My soul for rest, for my inspiring Guide
Bore me to vaster visions day by day.

My eyes had seen the Cromwell host revive
The rose of purity in our fair land,
I saw a warrior with his armour on
Find innocent allurement in a child
As with a poet's fancy. Women knew
The soft protection of a gentler man
Than eye had seen or heart had known before,
Our babes inhaled the breath of sacred song;
Men saw more glory in their clinging love
Than in the thundering cannon-blast of war.
(More hope lies in a babe than in a man;
More flowers illume the valleys than the peaks
Of savage mountains desolate with storms,

More hope Beyond than in this troubled Day.)
Yet each man moved in fear.   One walked the land
With his loved Bible bound about his breast;
Another tossed afar all ghostly thought
And lived but for an hour's frivolity;
A third, wrapped in the mantle of the Church,
Created creeds and formulas and oaths
That all must follow or embrace Despair;
And so from this wild tempest-cloud of thought
The lightning came, war and the crash of arms;
And o'er the Atlantic in the furious foam
Sailed those grand souls who sought the Lord in peace;
While braver Cromwell 'mid his thousand foes
Cut his triumphant way thro' King and crowd
To the just government of all the land:
In all creative thought the good survives.

And now my Guide with passion in his breath
Opened to my delight a newer world :—

"Behold!" said he, "these Puritans have cast
A snowy whiteness o'er the nation's thought,
But in their zeal for righteousness they hide
The sun of sweetness from the flowery land.
To touch the harp and bid my country sing
Songs of deliverance from thrall of guilt
Is my great joy; and when I hear the strange,
Old chains of slavery clatter to the ground,
And I behold my England rising free
To face a gathering Continent of storm
New songs break from my lips just as the waves
Burst in their stormy grandeur o'er the shore!
Here could I sing how our great nation rose,
Crushed by her cruel kings, and took the crown
In her own trembling hands and placed it firm
Upon another princely brow, to wear
At a true people's pleasure, for the good

Of all, cultured by courtesy on high.
But the great time is past and there are yet
Wonders to be unfolded and retold : "—

Then in a moment through the crusted earth
We swiftly passed, as though it were no more
Impediment than ambient air ! and lo !
We to a chamber came that had been caved
Long years ago by some great spirit-hand
Using the lightning of the universe
Armed with imperious thunder.   And my thoughts
Flew back to that far day when that great cave
Was hollowed in the earth and hearts above
In palpitating fear heard subterranean
Wonder-sounds ; clung to the trees and felt
The moving land slip from their trembling feet
As though 'twere weary with its weight of man ;
And not a breathing brother ever dreamed
That spirit-fingers in the granite earth
Were working wonders for the babe unborn.
As in the keen drilled core wormed from the depths
We read earth's tales, so, as we entered earth,
I saw the strata in a hundred forms
Lit by our glowing spirits as we slid
Silently down.   Through peat, and glacial drift,
And coralline we went ; through limestone, coal,
Impervious clay and penetrable sand,
Chalk, and a hundred other varying forms
Of man's geology.   And, as we passed,
Behold I saw the tempting lode of gold
And flash of native silver, sights to woo
Pale man to venturous life for gorgeous gain,
And when we to the cavern came my eyes
Beheld my spirit-countrymen at work,
Ralph Page and Peter Baude recasting o'er
Our Sussex iron in a mould of clay,
And in the midst our giant Chancellor,

E

The learned Bacon, stood, born of those years
That cradled Shakespeare, whose poetic tongue
Was tipped with honeyed words by the sweet-fays
That haunt the blossoms in the Avon vales.
And as we gazed, lo! Bacon to my guide
Advanced with an obsequious step and smile:

" Hail! hail!" said he, " Welcome, thou spirit fair!
For in this cavern grew your hopes and mine,
'Twas here I found the spirits that had touched
The earth with science-figures; those who peered
Into the elements and mapped the ways
Of the surprising compound; froze the air
And brought it as a solid to my feet.
'Twas here I learnt the sweet reality
Of all the dreams that I had pictured in
My solemn tomes; and, now, so great the joy
In this ancestral hall, that, if God willed,
We might with our great knowledge recreate
His magic earth and all its kindred stars!
It is for warm Humanity we work
In whose bright forefront stand our countrymen.
A British baby born 'mid rocks and waves,
Cradled in barks alive with troubled steam,
Becomes a finer force by our great aid
Than Grecian Neptune with his trident proud
Blown o'er the Pagan waters of despair!
Our witchery made the pregnant eye of Watt
Find Force in steam, and shaped the dream of speed
To Stephenson, who now has belted earth
With the fine fabric of his mortal toil!
We flashed Light's testament on Newton's mind,
Bade him behold God's gravitating law
That holds Man's body in a grave of dust
Lest he may flit into Infinitude,
Buoyed into space by his aspiring soul:
Shewed him the unseen ribbon binding earth

To the great golden sun and that again
Unto a greater, till, in awe, the whole
Bespangled universe of stars he saw
Move slowly round the hidden thought of God
In silent glory, while our unit souls
Flit forth as birds on wondrous errands bent
From star to star! 'Twas Newton, too, who left
For man an untold heritage of wealth
Folded within the leaves of his "Principia."
And here, I met the alchemist of fame,
My namesake, Roger Bacon, who beneath
His friar's robe wrought wonders on the earth
Leaving in man's frail hands a power to blow
A blustering brother to eternity,
Or level low a mountain to the plain:
So that the gentle friar of peace became,
Unwittingly, the instrument of war,
And now we oft above this cavern hear
The deadly boom of Man's artillery,
His coward wrath blown from his cannon jaws,
While we in our laboratory test
The chemicals of earth and fling our fire,
Smoke, dust, and all the refuse of our toil
Through the dread funnel of Vesuvius;
So close our spirits are to matter born!"

At this my Guide turned to my wondering soul
And said:—"This glorious spirit-voice that speaks
Out of the halls of Time to thee was once
The all-inspiring dreamer of his age.
He pictured glories for the eyes unborn
And from the seed of his philosophy
Created Newton and the magic host
Who deck thy country's firmament and shine
As constellations to the praise of God.
These are the men who spake the herald thought
Into the wilderness, and bade thy race

Erect on earth the consecrated dome
Of Industry, making thy lovely land
The manufacturing genius of the world
In every ray of light lives Newton's name;
The lightning-flash proclaims a Faraday;
The bounding blood still pulses Harvey's thought
Through generations, e'en as brooklets tell
Their diamond rosaries in Nature's praise.
But lo! a lovelier, lowlier mind draws nigh,
Without whose aid thy country had not seen
The great world mirrored forth from day to day
Upon the silent page."
                         And, as I turned,
A strange old man, with serious eyes drew near
And leaned upon my shoulder, full of words :—

" I am the ancient Caxton, who became
The first great labour-saver of our realm,
For I taught type to multiply the word,
And put a weapon in the hands of man
Greater than all the cannon-breaths of war,
Or the great onrush of material suns
Through the vast ether of Infinitude."

And, as he spake, he in an instant changed
From one whose visage withered was with age
To an enchanted figure lit with glee,
Like sunlight leaping with the fairy morn
Over the peeping mountains Linked with him
Were Newton and ten other souls, whose eyes
Had read God's volumes of the Universe
The earth passed from us and each soul was changed
From dross of Matter into forms so fair,
That I could only with my spirit eyes
Discern their loveliness; and, as we flew
I felt a new-born joy thrill through my soul
A thrill that told me I was near the Mind

That wrought the unfolded pattern of the rose
Ere on earth's bosom its fair form betrayed
Its gentle Fatherhood (e'en as lilies tell
Of their sweet culture when they come to share
Man's multitudinous woe).   Lit with this Mind,
Like my great brother-minds, lo ! I beheld
The secret of all Life which on the earth
Had my dull eyes eluded.   Now I felt
The force of Nature in the Universe
Filling the Earth, the glowing suns, the stars,
With magic life ;—the magic of the Mind
That lives in All.   And, as this potent thought
Flooded my soul, our Newton, great with love,
Led all his clustering brothers and my Guide
And me to a fair peak that overlooked
Our happy Isles and there spake he these words :—

"Lo ! now we see the modern England rise,
Her lust slow dying as her righteous mind
Governs her gifted hand.   Kings may indeed
Silence a stormy continent of men
By the dread cannon-voice of war, but each
Proud empire, conqueror, king, or power
Must vanquished fall before the light of Thought.
(A stable throne enshrines a people's heart.
A tyranny dissolves as icebergs melt
In the warm waters of a temperate sea.)
So our fair England with instructive breath
Has taught her generations to die great,
Searching for knowledge in the wonder-scroll
Spread by the Almighty on the circling earth
And in the heavens."   Then, turning to my Guide,
He said :—"To thee, Great Spirit, I declare
My just and grateful homage ; but for thee
I might have wandered in the fields of earth
And seen Eve's apple fall with heedless eyes !
Led by thy hand the tutored South drew nigh

And touched my eyes with light, till thought grew clear
And I went hand in hand with God thro' all
His Universe.   I saw Him turn the earth
Until the zone of torrid splendour reached
The frozen poles, and there in death He laid
The bird enchanted woods, and bade the streams
And avalanches roll the mountains down
Upon them, till the patient centuries viewed
The tropic forest miracled in coal.
And o'er this hoarded magazine of wealth
In joy he placed thy enterprizing mind
To build Man's furnaces of working fire
That mould the metals into forms of life ;
Looms that with automatic fingers weave
The giant cable or the cobweb gauze ;
Levers that with a gentle touch uplift
A mass of matter as we poise a straw ;
Each one obedient to the skilful mind
That dowers it with the fabric of his dream,
E'en as the chemistry of earth and air
And the magnetic current thrilling man
Evolve the fine conception of the God
Who bade fair Spring herald His love with flowers.
Thus thy industrious fingers fashion forth
The will of Him who sanctifies Work's dream.
The Prince of Savages holds court with Death
E'en as the Prince of Culture, but the man
Who consecrates himself to hope in Work
Bows not to Death in fear, but in the grave
Reads the beginning of his work Beyond.
No morbid fear shallows a working mind.
Thus thou hast guarded well th' Almighty trust :
In every human centre of thy land
Great science spreads her wonders.   To thy wheels
She gives her force and speed, and bids them whirl
Thy industries afar to savage glen,
To cultured Court and central citadel,

And to thy brethren far beyond the seas !
And through the world's vast avenues ye spread
The language and the thoughts of mighty men
Who have been near to God.   O King !   O Slave !
O spirit of my race ! uplift the soul
Who fathoms out God's wonders, and who sees
How Reason regulates each kindled star,
And builds the magic palace of the Mind,
The flowers of Spring, the fruit, and then the seed,
And flings the dead leaves down to give anew
Vitality to earth !   O Spirit King !
Treasure that man whose heart thrills to the chord
That can but be resolved beyond the tomb,
For from his lips such ecstasy may flow
As shall be music for a million ears !
Behold ! great Spirit, how we toiled for thee !
See how the first small Viking boat has grown
Into the armed leviathan that scorns
The boisterous main and carries in his breast
So murderous a sting that naught but Death
May wait upon his foe.   See how his breath
Obscures the heaven with cloud ; list to his voice
Booming across the waters in his wrath ;
And watch his eye as through the dismal night
He glares around, each part of his great bulk
The last word said by Science to the world,
E'en as the perfect poet when he sings
Utters the varied wisdom of his age !
But further wonders yet the world shall see,
For in the great laboratory of earth
We with our yearning spirits yet pursue
The dreams that charmed our lives, when, like the
      Spring,
We shed our fresh conceptions to the world
And peeped into God's secrets ; and in time
The force that moves the planets may be thine,
The lightning, rain-cloud, wind and water thine,

And all the varying elements may obey
Thy pliant hand! But when such wonders come
Remember that no marvel under heaven
Can be compared to Man's unbounded mind;
The sun may fade, the earth may pass away,
Yet Man's quick joy of thought shall ever be
His greatest wonder As the rose from naught
Will blush its beauty to the morn, so Man
Rises through Death to altitudes of Life
But half-divined on earth. Therefore, be meek,
When in thy hand the elements are held
As a new robe, and know, that greater force
Lies in thy soul than in a tempest-cloud
Or in the sun! And to thy race we look,
We souls of heaven, to rouse to energy
The world of Man!"
                With this he ceased, and, then,
I to my Guide turned all my wondering eyes.
It seemed so like a dream yet it was real,
Real as the hills that like black giants frown
At silent heaven and the silent stars
When the great sun lies curtained in the night
Upon his pillowy bed of cloudy bloom
These ten great souls decked the proud vault of
     heaven
As perfect blooms from Britain's rosaries
Preserved for ever for our wondering eyes.

But, as I gazed, lo! Newton sped afar
With his ripe brothers, like great streams of light,
All on some wondrous occupation bent,
And we were left in darkness on the peak
That loomed in grandeur o'er our Saxon isles,
Where once King Arthur with unhappy eyes
Gazed on his crumbled kingdom ere he felt
His mundane body melt into the blue.
Then said my Guide :—"Now have thine eyes re-seen

How thy great fathers hover round the home
That on the earth they founded thro' their tears
And through the travail of their discontent,
That ever gives to fine emotion birth.
Behold ! behold their thought-inspiring rays ! "

And then I saw from a great altitude
The concentrated thought of these great minds
Poured on one sacred spot upon our Isles
Where dwelt a humble seeker after truth
Whose name I knew not, but the world shall know
In some pale annal found by future eyes
On kind discovery bent.   And I was grieved
To see the unobservant world roll round
This gifted man with its vain, noisy breath
Regardless of his holy industry.
(For never falls the concentrated ray
On him who mocks or scorns, but it is drawn
By intellectual yearnings hour by hour
To the most saintly mind ; blessing the bard
Who feels the shadowy magic steal in words
Into the rich elixir of his pen.)
Then my great Guide wrapped me within his arms
And soared with me to view, a larger field
Less shadowy than the ancient Past, yet more
Alive with wonder, and I pined to know
How I might consecrate with fitting words
These pictures passing o'er my dome of thought
Like stars that glorify the blue of heaven.

CANTO VII

We felt a thrill pass through ethereal space
As a majestic wave of mystic Thought,
Freighted with Hope, sped to the furthest world.
On earth pale Man was waking, for the times

Were harvesting the centuries of Christ
Twice nine in number, and His Passion moved
Through all the tongues of the English multitude.
Whitefield was as a fire and Wesley spake
The word of Righteousness to willing ears,
Rousing the people to the point of war
On Sin's insane dominion   As a bird
Cleaves the blue air, so my inspiring Guide
Bore me beyond the limits of the moon
To a fair watchful star, where I beheld
A multitude, whose souls had lived on earth
And passed in lingering love into the blue.
Lone emperors of icy solitudes
And sunny equatorial hearts were there,
Men like us all, born with a boundless mind,
Whose flight from earth is one aspiring dream.

Who can limn spirits to a mortal eye
Or paint a picture of the impalpable?
And yet I knew by some mysterious law
Each unit in the mighty multitude.
There was no sense of eye, or ear, or touch,
Yet each quick spirit read the open mind
Of him with whom he silently communed;
To use a tongue seemed true tautology.
Just as on earth in wonder we transmit
Electric messages from shore to shore
Through some uncanny medium in the air,
Or as we feel some silent Spirit speak
His firm commands into our inner ear,
So in that vast assembly flew swift thought
From soul to soul   And thus these millions came
Responsive to that memorable call
Which we had felt pass through the Universe
But there was one, who, from the farthest fringe
Of heaven came silently towards the throng,
Swift as the hissing fluid from a cloud,

Or as a comet witching the blue night
Of solar space.   And as the soul drew near
I saw it was the burning mind of one
Whose brow was crowned with Empire and whose
    hand
Was sceptred with authority, whose soul
Made slaves of all.   And in his train there came
A being bearing a portentous book
That seemed alight with glory, flashing forth
The colours that the artist-sunbeams paint
Upon the fairy architecture of the rain.
Towards this sceptred form the assembly bowed
Low with great homage, saying :—"Hail! O King!
Alfred, the mighty lord and founder fair
Of the great Saxon Empire!" Then he breathed
His majesty abroad and all the throng
Silently watched his bearer ope the book,
"The Anglo-Saxon Chronicle," which he
Had kept from his beginning; records rare
That all the multitude revered   But when
The leaves were parted by his magic hand,
As in a mirage on the earth we see
Strange pictured marvels, so to us appeared
The heroes to our modern history born;
Not in pale pride but flushed with love they came.

And first came William Pitt, the glorious Earl,
Who drew the Viking valour from our race
As the wise sun draws vapour from the sea.
He taught the British heart to scorn a bribe
And made our cannon-breath become the voice
Of a great nation, not the fevered force
Of discontented kings or their loose lords.
He seemed as an astrologer who reads
The written skies.   He trod not earth in fear
He took the kingdom by the hand and strode
Into the field of glory as a child

Gathers the king-cups on a summer's day.
And as he came, I said —"Behold ! I see
In this great soul the issue of our Past,
Courage and Strength and purity of aim
That had been slowly for a thousand years
Flowering to fruit.   Now, I behold, kind Guide,
Thy prophesy fulfilled "   And as I spake
I saw the statesman silent homage pay
To Alfred and his glorious company,
As from his lips fell forth these potent words :—

" I come at thy command, most mighty King.
I hear the sound of warring hosts on earth
As England's warriors dare Man's doom of Death,
Not for reward but for the weal of all :
A golden glory that no Hebrew, Greek,
Roman, or great Egyptian felt of yore,
A glory only to the Saxon born !
O, Alfred, my great King ! when man meets man
Armed with Time's new Titanic Science-power,
Woe to the hand that beats the drum of War.
Rather would I Heaven's cloudy batteries fire
Than wake Man's new intelligence to life !
Whereas of old the cruel sword but slew
The unskilful few, such wonders have been won
From the worn centuries of Thought that now
A touch may hurl an avalanche of souls
Into the abyss of Death and fill with forms
The curtained theatre of Life Beyond.
Had I the marshalling of the nations now,
Slow would I be to move, but, if I moved,
I   would   so   storm   the   world   that   fear   should
      bind
All Saxon peoples in a league of peace
Which no barbarian elements might break
While the great league breathed Christ-born
      Righteousness."

And while he spake these words a magic sea
Before us in a ferment seemed to roll.
Then brilliant streamers from the deep arose
Such as on Winter evenings we behold
When angels light th' Aurora at the poles ;
And they were shaped as a vain peacock shapes
His fairy fan to win admiring eyes.
(Newton, who knew the secrets of the Light
Bade it unfold these wonders.)   Then there came
Slowly upon the sea a ship of war
Belted with steel,—vessels men build on earth
To spread abroad a desolating name,
In irony of what the angels choired
Twenty long, dunceful centuries ago.
And on its prow, bowing with noble mien,
I saw the silent orator who breathes
His valorous virtue forth in granite form
In the Valhalla of Trafalgar Square,
Where every British heart may view in love
Some sacred lineaments of our warrior-peers,
Voiceful as violets that in Spring-time sing
Of a Creative Presence who has left
His grace on earth.   For of what need God's flowers
Unless the eye of man their message read ?
And of what force these monuments in stone
Unless the spirit that uplifted them
Breathe in the hearts around ?   Both stone and flower
Without Man's love tell but of Man's decay,
Like the dark dust of silent Nineveh.

This valiant Nelson, like the inspiring sun,
Illumed the sea with splendour, and his voice
Clove through the air amid the observing host,
As waves break in glad glory on the shore,—
This great tumultuous soul that never dies :—

" Alfred, my King ! and all ye Lords of Thought !

Who roused the energy of my race to forge
This engine of destruction, list to me!
If now I breathed on earth, and fain might wake
This instrument to life, the world would hear
Of such heroic wonders that the Past
With all its noble pictures would become
As children's gentle mummery of war
So great this new destructive that 'twill make
A mighty mausoleum of my sea!
When I and my charmed men in our rude halls
Held sport with Chance and tossed the dice with
     Death,
And quaffed with him the wine of Life,—tho' oft
He dashed the glittering goblet down,—full well
We knew that courage won the stakes. No more
May this be true, for now a coward may,
Armed with a science-wonder, blast a fleet
To air and top a monument of praise!
Like the diffusive splendour of the sun
My country rises on the wondering world
All the stored wealth and lessons of the Past
Combine to make her rising wonderful.
Not in the clouded palace of conceit
Is she content to live, but in the face
And criticism of the world, bidding
The humorous and satiric wind search through
Her branches of the Tree of Life to vent
Its healthy scorn. O that I now once more
Might helm her Navy through the seething sea
Of maddening Jealousy breaking round her shores!
But that can never be. My task is done.
Yet can we with a planned, united power
Pour down our spirit on our new-born race,
That every unit of new time may be
Strong as the noble captains of the Past
And every captain so exceed the old
That each new leader may be as a god,

Lifting with magic influence all the world,
So that the twentieth century may dawn
Upon a wise and bright humanity."

With this he ceased holding his ship in air ;
Proud in our growing pride.   Then, from afar,
I watched a red line slowly wend its way
Towards our concourse, just as a ribbon seems
Moved by illusive fingers in the blue
Upon a windy day, and, as it neared,
I saw, in love, the British hearts who shed
Their valour on the fields of Waterloo
To write Britannia's will on Europe's plains ;
And at their head rode the great Wellington
Who jewelled " Peace " in Queen Victoria's crown
And made the arm of Freedom known and felt
In the dull consultations of the proud.
At a mute motion from the King, the magic host,
Like a red garland twined around their Chief,
And every ear craved silence for the sound
Of his great voice :—
                    " Emperors and Lords of Thought !
I come," said he, " to bid Great Science halt,
Ere it betray the secret elements
To the brave minds who play the game of War
Upon the chess-board of the World.   No eye
Can see the wild explosive shell wound weak
Humanity and drop not Pity's tear.
I, with a blaze of War upon my breast,
Come to thy presence to protest my fears.
In might of dynamite the heroic dies.
Better flit back to proud Thermopylæ
And hold the pass of Freedom 'gainst the world
With a few brave than with a cruel shell
Silence a thousand tongues.   Men are as gods
Armed with the lightning, with no godlike power
To hide behind the battlements of heaven.

They have assumed too great prerogative.
If Man need War let him the Victor be
Who with the wand of courage strikes the foe
And claims the ribbon of nobility !
Of old we called no blood-stained butcher brave.
But, for my countrymen, I have no fear.
I know that they 'gainst fiery rain from Hell
Would stand as life-guards o'er high Principle,
And dash to death him who would harm the good
Or riot 'gainst the silent laws of God
Writ on the soul.   They who Napoleon stayed,
For Freedom and the general good of all,
Will still withstand the tyrant breed of Man,
Whate'er his guns may thunder !   Now the hour
Sounds in the belfry of the Universe,
When the new members of our race on earth
Must in one league be bound to fend the Right
And turn the lamp of Light on the dark world.
I feel the tempest hidden in the air ;
The stealthy feet of Treason haunt the night,
I, from my watch-tower, spy the spears of War,
Therefore, great Alfred, King, and Lord of all
Who wave the flag of Freedom, rouse to arms
All our vast spirit-millions at thy call,
And let us bind our new-born sons on earth
In one Imperial brotherhood of peace,
Unbreakable by any but themselves."

I heard these words with fear, but to my Guide
They came as come the voices of the Morn ;
They bodied forth his life, his faith, his dream ;
And then King Alfred said :—

                "Great Wellington !
And all ye souls who hold in thy strong hands
The future generations of thy race,
Take heed to me !   I was a warrior born.
Like thee I held sword-virtue in my hand,

Like thee I used it well.   But why bewail
The mighty onrush of the centuries
When Man seems walking in the steps of God,
Capturing His lightnings and holding converse
With His martial thunder.   If war be just
And thousand bodies die, we spirits know
That a kind hand weighs down with gold of Love
The scale wherein the war-made martyr stands
Before Almighty God in His pure heaven,
And sweet adjustments are by Justice given.
If War be just and Man be lifted high
Above the world on wings of Principle,
Of what account the heap of buried bones
If but the spirit-heights be won, and Man
May gaze at Truth as at a sunrise-dream,
And live in ecstasy with the Unknown.
And let none say that Man must not be scourged
By Righteousness if he forsake the Truth
And live in languorous luxury and die
Unmindful of the living light around !
Tell me,—what weapon has the Almighty forged
For the arm of a righteous nation but grim War ?
Mercy is but the kindly kiss of him
Who stands victorious and whose heated breath
Might flame destruction !   So, in Peace, would I
Bid all my new-born brothers fathom forth
Earth's most rebellious secrets, till, in time,
No savage mind shall mould a curse on earth
And no contagious enemy cry war !
For all shall learn what we have learnt since
      Death,
And the embodied souls on earth shall move
Safely as planets in the plains of heaven
Within God's holy and imperious laws.
To this great consummation let us call
The spirit-ancestors who built our Past,
And let us as one spirit circle earth,

F

And pass our message to our race, as joy
Beams through the silent sunbeam on a flower."

Then, once again, on Speed's electric wings
I felt majestic messages fly forth,
And I beheld a multitude appear
In silent wonder from the silent Past;
And great King Alfred marshalled every soul
In serried order, till the magic host
Spread forth before me like a moving sea
Of palpitating life.   Each instant brought
New ardent souls released by Death to head
The aspiring van, and, then, in ordered years
Were ranged the ancestral millions, till the rear
Tapered away to those first yearning few
Who planted their free feet on British ground.

As on a solemn evening one may see
The holy twilight dyeing dark the green,
While massed battalions gather in the clouds,
So seemed that scene to me.   And then it moved,
Pressing with all the wisdom of the Past,
Into the unborn Future undeterred.

As though the martial mind of Homer lived
And breathed poetic breath among my people,
(Glad at great deeds, gladder at great thought,)
So in grand song that congregation joined.

Then, like a phosphorescence on the sea,
Divine effulgence from that throng was thrown
Upon our dreaming Isles, for it was Night
On earth.   I saw my sleeping countrymen
In miracle the silent host receive
Into their souls; some felt the pageant pass
As a memorial dream, while others deemed
The magic presence but the rising moon

As they on wakeful pillows watched its rays
Steal o'er the coverlet in silvery shades,
Or beat a silver pathway o'er the waves
To lead their Senses to the Beautiful.
Thus the bright Vision of Material eyes
Dazzles away the Spirit-palaces
That rise in shadowy outlines in our brains
And at a touch of Science fall away!

I turned enquiring to my guide, but he
Still bade me gaze; and then my eyes beheld
The gathered cloud of spirits glide as one
Around the sleeping world, led by the King.

And first o'er wide America they passed,
Where a proud heritage of British hearts
Had built the Great Republic of the Free;
Then over Canada the spirits flocked
Where a new race of Freemen look to Heaven,
Linked by warm love to courteous royalty;
Then flew they o'er the far New Zealand isles,
Where the new majesty of Britain lives
In loyal hearts; then o'er Australian plains
Where every soul who treads its golden paths
Is a true freeman born; then to the North
They flew, skirting the China sea, where live
Our countrymen, who, year by year, in peace
Knock wonderingly at the Celestial door;
Then glided they where the great Ganges pours
Mercy's wise tears from Himalayan snows,
(Frost-crowns by angel fingers placed upon
Those giant janitors of Hindustan;)
And back they swept again to Burma, where
Strange Buddha poured his sleepy gospel deep
Into the pulsing arteries of the people;
From thence they flew to magic Africa,
Where holy Livingstone reposed his bones

While fathoming the thoughts of alien hearts ;
Then o'er old Egypt, where the Pharaohs laid
Their mummies in memorial Pyramids ;
Past Malta and Gibraltar and the gates
Of martial peoples ; but, where'er they flew,
They poured in love their magic message down
Upon the Saxon people spread afar
Amid the complex nations ; then they fled
Before my eyes into the Great Unseen.

And I was dazed at our vast influence ,
The very corners of the earth seemed held
In Saxon hands   We seemed to stream abroad
Like little rivulets of mercury
Alert for gold, gauging the heat and all
The wind and weather of the world.   Great souls,
Who, had they entertained the martial wish,
Might have conceived a tropic-world of slaves ;
But it was Peace, not War, kind Freedom's rule
That spread our Saxon glory through the world !

Once more I wondered to my guide, but he
Still bade me gaze, and, then, I saw afar
A brilliant Light blot out the stars of heaven,
Just as they fade before the sun at morn.
Kingdoms, archangels, all immortal souls,
Celestial hierarchies, knowledge, power, and thought,
Were all contained in that absorbing Light,
And, though I saw no Form or tender Eye,
I heard a Voice that said :—
                              " O earth-born Man !
O Saxon-yearner for the highest !   What
Art thou?   Hast thou but butterfly delight?
What thy conception of the stars that gleam
Far from the touch of thy fingers ?   If to thee
Be given the power to uplift the world
Wilt thou be true?   Or wilt thou, brutelike, seek

To lure thy fellows in a web of scorn,
And on them prey with spiderlike ambition?
We fear for thee as for the mighty minds
Who quelled the Past and saw their feeble arms
Decay e'en while they ruled! And yet we hope.
For thou art the conception of our Mind,
Free to ascend or fall as thou shalt choose!
Our light doth live in thee! Shouldst thou conceive
Defiance of our laws, then must thou die!
The triumph is to Righteousness alone,
Christ-taught, by Love, on Calvary!
A nation rises but to fall that strives
For mere possession, as though men were stones
Or valued mire. They pulse, like thee, with Love,
Or blaze with Hate. To our all-patient Mind
The Christian and Mohammedan are one,
The Jew and Gentile but like blades of grass
That seek eternally the light above.
Then if to thee, O Saxon! we convey
The power to raise thy brothers to the beams
Above the sun, wilt thou be true, wilt thou
Be honourable, and on Temptation wage
Love's glorious war? If so, to thee, O race
Whom we have reared, we grant the giant task!
The hosts of heaven shall speed thy destiny,
For when Man's mundane eye on God may gaze
Then shall the Bible of the Universe
Be writ for all creation, and each world
Shall learn the history of Man on earth
To teach its generations to be free,
For Freedom breeds the highest and the best.
Clanship is dead; Kingship is but a name,
An emblem of a people; Patriotism,
With all its selfishness, must die! The world
Is now man's common heritage , a wrong,
Though it have unction from the Papal Hand,
Shall to a rich rebellion rouse the world;

And thou shalt be its leader : by all tongues
Thy language shall be breathed, till 'tween the realms
Of Arctic and Antarctic all shall thrill
With simultaneous thought, upleading to
The great consolidation of Mankind."

Then silence and dead darkness, till the stars
Once more revealed their gentle place on high,
For the loved earth still hid the sleeping sun.

But I was conscious that the spirits came
Nearer to earth, than when of old I saw
The angel-cross flutter above our Isles,
When Peter and his Christian company
Wrought the bright emblem in the firmament
As a cloud-bloom of crimson, cream, and gold,
At the first dawn of Saxon unity.

Then to my Guide I turned, and, weeping, said :—
"Can my loved country such a mission bear ?
Are her wise lips persuasive ?   Can she chant
With ecstasy unto another land ?
Can she woo wisdom from a proudling State
That arms itself with cannon-arguments,
And makes of its male millions soldier-slaves,
As though there were in every gusty wind
Clarion alarms of War ?
                    Then said my Guide,
With earth-ward gaze :—"Behold, how gardener Time
Delves knowledge from the dust !   Eden has gone ;
That first poetic Paradise of Man ;
But Eve remains, entrancing as of old,
By Britain and America made free.
No longer dolls of discord but the Rose-
Princesses of the realm, the Violets
Of Freedom ; sunny garlands crowning Man.
And now each new-born Adam and new Eve

Looks on no land with avaricious eyes
But would a world-wide Eden make in peace
Without the thought of a Forbidden Tree !
But lo ! Time's lessons hurry from the dust."

Swiftly wild clouds blurred the blue firmament
Passing our faces like weird winding-sheets
That drape the dead.   Then, suddenly, upon
The great white veils aërial pictures flamed
That drew me from the realms of heaven to earth,
Where Man was toying with the rose of Life
With feverish fingers.   In the East I saw
A lazy populace on poppied beds,
Their earth-life lapped in dreams ; but in the West
I saw a cultured king from a gold throne
Felled by hysteric hands, as, womanlike,
France gasped at the high breath of Liberty,
And grew intoxicated with the breath,
And trampled in her zeal her cultured down,
Till Freedom changed to license unrestrained,
Rolling in conflict over Europe's plains
With mad Napoleon of the tempest-crowd,
Offspring of Revolution's fiery womb ;
The strange mesmeric magic of whose mind
Entranced a pliant people, even as drones
Exact a tribute from their busy world.
I shuddered as I gazed, for I beheld
Humanity ablaze.   They would have seared
Each other at a touch, but a Wise Hand,
Outstretched from heaven, armed our great race for
      War,
And stamped the human conflagration down
'Neath the Teutonic wrath of Waterloo.
All these wild sights I saw.   Then there was Peace,
Sweet occupation of my busy race,
Forging the quick machinery of the world,
Framing the viaduct from crest to crest

To leap across the valleys at a bound,
And spanning floods with cantalever beams
That seem upheld by angel arms from heaven;
Building the chest to hold the breath of Steam
And tongue of Fire,—those potent slaves of Man
That have the Nineteenth Century's chariot wheels
Hurried towards the Infinite. I saw them speed
With dazzling wake of snow-white foam across
The ocean of the Lord and o'er His land
With a revolving fury whirling night
And day, like His great wheel of Earth, till the East
Was as the West and Space and Time as naught,
And Man rose Master o'er the elements
I saw an emperor of magic grasp
The fleeting air and 'neath his cunning hand
Compress it to a solid of such power
That it rebuked its maker and became
The wonder-child of Science. Then I heard
A breath of blasphemy against the Book
Where God inscribed His love-lit Righteousness.
Science had with unphilosophic hand
Blotted the page and blurred the sacred light
That shone on all men from Creation's eyes;
Forgetful that their own new mental lore
May to the Science yet unborn become
False as the sun-halt before Joshua,
Or the old fixity of Mother Earth.
And I heard Priests fend their dear Book in pride,
Blind as their censors, for they never dreamed
That God was writing His eternal Book
Upon the tablets of each giant mind
That wakes the world with wonder, while they drone,
Placidly faithful to a faithless Faith
Ivied in ruined grandeur o'er its Creeds.

But I was proud to see scene after scene
Breathe forth the Resurrection royalty

Of Love-crowned Christ, with whom each Briton
    walked
Unconscious, ofttimes, of the Regal Shape
That in his shadow moved, while still, the Priest,
Chattering of creeds and curses, ne'er perceived
The sweet, rebuking Presence moving all.
Christ in our Parliament invoked the realm
To march in glory through the world, fearless
And free   And I beheld our Senators
Planning the golden steps that upward lead
To the far vision and the unbounded dream.
To speak of one, 'mid many wonderful,
Would be a derogation of the rest.
They towered above their fellows as the sun
Leaps high above the earth, but, like the sun,
They shone their blessings down, and changed the
    land
From old to new, quick as poetic Spring
Buds into flower and loveliness and joy.
The base decrees of kings were all interred
Within their vaulted sepulchres, and men
With love-made laws lived holy lives and moved
Into the mansions of eternity.
Barriers were broken down, the nobles passed
Over the bridge of Love into the midst
Of toiling millions and became as guides
Of culture to the multitude.   And now
A new nobility surrounds the throne
Drawn from the complex millions of our realms.
I saw Love open all the prison doors
And claim the criminals as brother men ,
And then sweet Charity bewitched the land
And with her tears drew drops of gold from all,
Wherewith to bless the blind, and build the home
For him who is unconscious of himself ;
To heal the wounds of all mortality
So far as helpful brothers Christs may be.

Then, as in contrast to this pictured peace,
I saw wild, bloody interludes of war,
War not of our conceiving, but by Hate
Thrust on our land to test our righteous Pride ;
While we from our strong cannon's breath but breathed
Our principles,—free entry of the foot
Of man where'er his brother holds dominion,
Free intercourse, free trade, free thought, free speech ;
And, as I gazed, I saw the keys of earth
Were handed to Britannia of the Seas.

The cloudy grandeur left us like a dream
And silently we looked into the stars
And wondered what the Almighty had conceived
Behind the Twentieth Century's gorgeous veil.

CANTO VIII

THEN came a scene more magic far than all,
There was great argument in the wild sky,
Clouds with a voice of thunder woke the morn,
Stars fell, and in their fiery flight
Bore a great throng of spirits to our Isles.
I wondered at the music blown abroad :
A sacred choral from unnumbered tongues
Echoed from world to world, but, on the earth,
The magic music fainted in the trees
Dying away in dim immensities,
(As come dream-visitors to us at night
And in the cloak of morning glide away).
I was as one enchanted : not a breath
Passed unrewarded , every moment brought
Some rich consignment to my eyes and ears.
Just as at sunset a soft magic steals
Into our being and we love to feel
Each glowing colour stain our inner soul,

So felt I in that hour.   But I was not
As one who bids his wizard senses run
In riot o'er his soul ; my mind was tense
As his who feels the algebraic figures course
In crystal clearness o'er his cultured brain,
And firm and conscious as the prince of wise
Logicians on the earth ; so that no scorn
May to my testimony lend a sneer ;
For I saw not abstractions, but the deep,
Dark, inner sense of all-absorbing life.

Again King Alfred from the central heaven
Came like a sun, crowned, and in regal robes,
With spirits in his train whose forms had passed
From British realms into the realms unseen ;—
An unimagined multitude.   Our earth
Below, seemed waiting for the breath of God,
As waits the bard for efflorescent words,
Patient as Spring in his loved ecstasy.
The ferment glowing in Man's fertile heart
Thrilled me as with a fear, and suddenly,
The waiting mass broke into wildest war,
And on the tumbling Thought-waves of the world
My Soul was borne.   The human conscience seemed
Ablaze with life, and, like the facets on
A diamond shone, as from conflicting suns.

The unseen spirit orchestra, above,
Unheard by Man struck earth's great chords of Life ;
The wild vibrations thrilled from world to world,
'Till through the firmament vast millions came
To view the evolution of Mankind,
Deeming the twentieth century of Him
Who wrought the legendary Rose of Love
Would, in its train, bring forth the Car of Peace.
Then in the presence of those millions moved

King Alfred o'er a carpet of white clouds
Towards my Guide, saying, with joyful tongue :—

"O, Spirit of my Race ! the hour has come
When on the world thy soul must work its will,
Till Justice, Love, and Liberty shall be
The sunny heritage of all mankind."

On earth, though no ear heard or eye perceived,
Yet were all people with those feelings thrilled
That streamed in music thro' the dome of sky
And surged in glory to the furthest star,—
For naught divides the heaven from the earth
Save the partition of the Palpable.
All English hearts responded to that song ;
But the slaves of men, not born in Freedom's bower,
Felt their cramped hearts beat scorn ; (scorn that
     ne'er kills
The scorned but only cuts the scorner).   I,
Feeding on Hope, gazed on the human throng,
And pictured wonders breaking through the gloom.

King Alfred and our spirit-ancestors
Looked Southward o'er our Isles and saw the earth
Spread as a plain before them, (for our Thought
Views Matter as a dream and may compress
Into the hollow of the hand the whole
Vast area of stars in Science particles ;)
And on this level plain each nation seemed
As chess-men on the chequered board, as pawns
Moved by the fingers of the Hand Unseen !
To the West, laved by the blue Atlantic foam,
Lived legions of our race, fearless of foes,
Viewing the world with Love's pictorial eyes,
But to the South an alien nation held
Dominion o'er the vineyard of the world,
Brightly impulsive as their wine.   I should need

A battery of artillery to proclaim
In rightful voice the arrogance of their scorn
Aimed at the spreading splendour of our realm.
South-Eastward; lo! the dark dissecting brain
Of German brothers theorized and dreamed,
While their bound bodies drew the car of War.
And Eastward moved the Russian with his Serfs
And stormy Slavs, ever in clouds of gloom
And batteries of threatening wrath arrayed.

Though each great kingdom simulated Peace,
The pointed bayonet o'er each boundary line
Pricked terror in the true perceiving eye.
Each country from the year's incoming wealth
Hard tribute took, love-yielded from the soil,
And gave it to the gunner and the gun,
To camp and bastion, ambulance and sword,
As though poor man were of a panther born,—
A memory of a reptile,—and each king,
And costly Czar, and President but filled
A place of fear to fright his neighbour's eyes!

A brother ape of the Darwinian past,
Marketing mellow nuts from Autumn trees,
Feeling his god move in his phantom breath,
Might gaze in wonder at a martial man
And scorn to win his dull medallion's praise,—
A glory glutted with his brother's gore!

Ah! how our ancestors in Heaven's proud choir
Wept to behold these arsenals of Death
Taunting fair Freedom with black cannon-breath!
The merry may-buds laughing through the valleys,
The branches bursting with glad leaves and flowers,
The rose-buds blushing through the threatening
    thorn,
The corn-fields glowing 'neath electric suns

Were to our spirit-ancestors as breath,
So were the fine flung fancies of the Mind,
But these deep dark delusions bred sweet tears!

This vain conception of the throne of Power,
This little glory of the white-born Man
Who strutted with his rifle through his field
Scorning, conceitedly, the barbarous black,
Who, with the self-same martial fingers flung
The ready stone from the impelling sling,
Spread vast impatience in the souls on high.

Then from the towering heavens I beheld
A golden meteor unfold its joy.   It broke
Among the angel-millions as the sun
Breaks through the cloudy temple-veils of earth
To kiss its flowers   I gazed with happy eyes,
Thrilled with the heart-throbs of the multitude,
And in the meteoric splendour I
Beheld the Lord of Life, the Christ of crowns
Thorn-gathered on the earth, but now arrayed
In robes as bright as diamonds dancing in
The dazzling dew.   Through the great throng he
      moved
Until he stood the central force of all,
Weaving their minds around him as the sun
Entwines the planets in a web of love
Woven by Almighty hands.   No eye of earth
The mystic lineaments of the soul may see;
Else might I tell how Christ's forgiving gaze,
O'er-brimmed with sorrow, spread divinity
Abroad, as babes and flowers.   Each rival star
Brought its contingent multitude of souls
Until a galaxy of glory spread
Around Him o'er innumerable miles.
But near Him stood in courtesy of place
Those who had moved mankind to mirth or tears :—

Adam of Paradise, and Eve who soiled
The innocence of sweet obedience;
Noah, the navigator of the Flood;
Pharaoh and Joseph, ministers of Dreams;
Moses, the council-mind of magic Law;
Hector, the holiest heart of Ilium,
Achilles, burnished with the blaze of War,
And by their side the trumpet-bard who vaunts
Their fame for ever through the aisles of Time,
There, too, were ranged the architects of Tyre,
Founders of Nineveh and Ascalon,
Baalbec and Babylon, with those who reared
Man's early vestibules of sacred thought
In Athens, and Byzantium, and Rome;
Yea, all were there that ever had been born,
E'en strange Gautama, Christlike but for sleep,
But there was one more honoured than the rest,
The protestant of God 'gainst Pagan pride,
The saint of Grecian lore, sweet Socrates,
Who to polytheistic priests had shewn
The fluttering immortal in a man,
For he had touched the strange Invisible
In the dark, dreamful splendour of his mind,
And, therefore, from the martyr's hemlock draught
Had floated luminous to the Sublime,
The great thought fashioning the great deed done.
(So the true Artist dreams his Beauty-dream
Conscious, with the Artificer of Wealth,
That the wrought treasure and the tear of toil
Can never freighted be from earth, though he,
With but the naked magic of himself,
Seeks the great citadel of the Unseen.)

Beneath this vast assembly, (now so great
That e'en the outspreading firmament of stars
Vied not with it in splendour,) we beheld
The soaring earth wrapt in ascending flames

That yearned towards the Son of Righteousness
As lilies to the light.   They rose in wild
Effulgence, sea-like and tumultuous,
Grand as the vision of the sun when he
Ere dying in his shroud sheds o'er the heavens
His heart's warm ecstasy and charms the trees
And hills and clouds into sublimity.
Then said my Guide, lord of my questioning eyes :—

" Behold these flames are not of Matter born
For they are the corona of the thought
Of the great nations peopling earth ; But see!
The Anglo-Saxon flame o'erleaps the rest
In crown-like majesty ! "
                            With these true words
He glowed in conscious pride, while, as I gazed,
I felt the ascending and descending Mind
'Tween heaven and earth fill me with sacred fear.
Around, above, beneath our glorious Christ
And the selected few of winnowing Time
The angel-millions ranged, until He stood
The centre of a living orb of souls
Waiting to hear the treasury of his tongue
As lovers listen for the nightingale.
Ev'n as on Autumn evenings one may see
A fluttering crowd of birds form and reform,
As though at some imperious command,
So moved this multitude.
                            Long since my heart
Had lost the memory of its beats.   I breathed
No more.   From mortal to immortal changed,
Clothed with the astral-body of St Paul,
I in that wall of spirit faces felt
A wild, unbounded, irrepressive joy
Not of mortality ; and when I saw
The hushing hand of our great Christ arise,
Like sunshine o'er a storm, I felt the calm

Pass o'er the sea of faces, and the strange
Sweet music of His mind melt in us all.
This is my faint remembrance of His words :—

"Brethren of Earth! ye who once longed in flesh
For the fair freedom of the boundless blue,
I come to welcome thee on this great day
When Man proclaims my twentieth century!

I saw the earth flung from the hand of God ,
Saw the first Morning break and the first Night
Dazzle the firmament with silver stars ;
Beheld the Almighty teach the magic sun
To weave its changeful continent of clouds
And dip them deep in red or molten gold,
Dark purple, green, or any gorgeous hue
Of even varying wonder ; I saw His hand
Scatter the seed upon the ready ground,
And lo, the land returned His love with flowers ,
Great trees grew at his touch and the deep sea,
Secretly moving to the silent moon,
Obeyed His laws through hurricane or calm
And ever laved His love around the land.
And I saw God's great spirit bring forth Man
'Mid beasts and fish and fowl innumerable ;
And the activity of earth was as
The working of the furnace of His mind ;
And I beheld Man fall,—not that his gifts,
Unfitted to his state, bade him despair,
But that he chose to walk the verdant earth
As though it were his promenade of pride ;—
He tossed the laws of God in his free mind
As paltry playthings of his intellect. '
He said :—' If God made Evil in my heart
Then is he less than God ; I would not with
A devil dower my doll ; nor would I make,
Were I Omniscient, a mind like mine

G

That would invade my knowledge and reduce
My power.' Such trivial reasoning heard I pass
Down the tongue of Man's ages, and he longed
To live as though no Justice reigned at all!
Then, as ye know, I came The world was sown
With maxims of perfection, yet were they
Trodden down as worthless weeds. God's light I
Shed upon them 'till they bloomed and budded
Beauty in Man's fields of woe. So that now,
Soft-whispering like God's fairy flowers, my words
Are murmured by the lips of all. Man feels
The moral forces of the Universe
Sweeping in endless passion through his soul;
The mind-waves of the innumerable millions of the
      Past
Bear him rejoicing through Thought's silent sea,
He feels the Fatherhood that made him Man
In every new-born image of his flesh;
And now each baby-footstep moves inspired
By the sight of God in the lily and the rose,
In the electric forces of the sun,
In the quaint map engraven on the moon,
In doubtful nebulæ and passionate stars
And in the princely Reason of his mind
That shews how Goodness must with Evil dwell;
How birdlike Hope must hover o'er Despair;
How Pain impels Man to the righteous deed
When blundering roughly against Nature's laws;
How Sorrow threads its fine embroidery
Through all the raiment of the Soul he wears!
Yet see! ye universal millions! how
Thy earth-held brethren still refuse in fear
My sunny smiles of Love for frozen frowns.
Hear how earth's bishops torture God with prayers
For victory to their country's barbarous arms
As though the Deity rode in thunder-clouds
And bathed in blood Love's mantle of the Morn!

Yet these earth-senators of God know well
That we departed millions wait in love
For Man's great resurrection of the Soul,
Wait to behold the slave-chains of his flesh
Fall to the ground, that he may once more be
Free as God made him, innocently free!
But this all ye assembled millions know.
And now the clock of Time sounds the great hour
For which my centuries have waited. Man,
Aglow with the effulgence of the Past,
Front-lit with suns of Hope, exalts his soul
Until the heart of Self doth in him die,
Though Pain shall still be teacher as of old
And Grief his close acquaintance. Love shall charm
All his creative thought and move his hand,
For now out of the dust of nations, I
My Anglo-Saxon children rouse to life,
They glow with Me e'en as the sun in love
Glows in the flowers. Crude are they in their love,
Like a rude man in cultured company,
Yet would their souls assimilate high Heaven,
And in the luxury of Love lead Man
Through labyrinthian Thought to God: Behold!
Behold! Man's mighty change!"
                    Then, as a dream,
Before my eyes the vast blue Future rolled
Like a wide threading sea. The tiny scenes
Of earth far faded in the glowing Past,
My ancestors as pigmies were, whose little souls
Had lived their trivial enterprize and died.
All things were new. The stars were but as rocks
In the empyrean of blue where souls,
New charmed by Christ, had their unbounded
     home,
And I was one of that imperial throng,
And, with enchanted eyes, as we read books,
Read my first volume of Eternity.

My Guide and I lived in the breath of God
The Inaccessible, and yet the Force
That vitalizes all, setting the blood
Of kings and potentates in motion,
Who, with a touch, might stay the pulse of all
And reign in Silence 'till His thought again
Break into new creation !   I was awed
With all the solemn sanctity around
And longed for rest, but still my Guide toiled on,
Unfolding greater wonders to my eyes.

CANTO IX

THERE lay the Future like a sleep-held town
Waiting for stir of Day !   The things to come,
The uncreated Man, the Soul to be
Stood aching for the touch of Life, and I,
Lured by my Guide, looked on with face of fear.
Just as Man's weird imagination wakes
The story dormant in his magic brain,
So on that silent scene the breath of God,—
The Unseen Influence,— played.   Our *lensèd* eye
Saw naught of these strange things   Another Sense,
Far finer than the cellular-millioned brain's,
Came to our aid, and with that Sense we gazed
Into the destinies of glowing worlds !
What strange Orion or Arcturus held
In their great orbs we sought not to discern ,
We left the Vast unfathomed, unexplored,
Though the unfolded Vision charmed our mind
As when at night Man dreams into the stars ;
But for the Earth our hearts beat ecstacy
As we beheld the working of God's mind.

We saw the magic Future rise to life
Unfolding like a flower, but God made not

Soul-soaring Man a dull automaton ;
He had but pre-ordained a Principle,
A rule of Life, as from the sea and sun
He weaves a cloud and from the cloud the rain,
No drop the same though of one pattern formed.
So, as a Father, for His child, the Man,
He had ordained the rule of Righteousness.
The individual was free to pulse
Along the line of "least resistance," but,
Battering with scorn each fine philosophy,
Man ever cuts his Pain-protected bones
Against the crags of Wrong, shunning the neat
And easy paths of Rectitude ! A cloud
Of silken summer sun is heaven's delight,
A rose a maid's fond folios of Love,
A man of Righteousness, God's ecstacy!

So as the Future dawned, we saw no man
Who was, like set machinery, preconceived,
Each unit grew, moulded and chastened by
Earth's calm and storm. God never planned the
      bruise
Upon a flower though He ordained the law
That brought the tempest-torment from the skies.

But while embroidering my recipient mind
With these philosophies, I felt my Guide
Rouse me to life as each new soul uprose
Partly pre-ordinated. Then I saw
That from my happy country came the thought,
The action and the men that stirred the world.
Against them stood rebellious elements ;
Each Briton rose oblivious of his foes.
They were as naught to him ; he looked afar
Beyond the sky-line of his circumstance ;
And to my Guide I said :—
                "Behold ! thy dreams,

Which once I scorned, are now as life to me.
The race that can forget its race and merge
Its millions in the rest, not for mere gain
But for the glory and the good of all,
Must be for all a blessing."
                    And my Guide,
Made happy by my words, raised me to heights
That Thought had never traversed ; shewed me scenes
That mortals may not picture, and in fear
I bade him all his mystic truth imprint
Upon the canvas of my brain.   Then I saw
Four models of our tremulous orb appear,
Sudden conceptions of God's plastic mind,
Such as he whirls into the chart of heaven
When magic nebulæ flash forth and die,
Waking Man's wonder !   And the orbs were named
The worlds of Love, Hate, Death and Indifference,
Their Evolution based on riddle Man.
And as we gazed on actual Earth we saw
How easily might mortal Man transform
His working world to one of these clear four !

When Homer threw his mind into the heavens
And gazed upon his gods how glad was he !
So I upon these wonders looked with joy.
They were four lessons from the Almighty flung
Into observing Space to teach my Guide
And me the possible in Man, the height
And depth of his attainment ; and I felt
How our inheritance might slip away
If with an easy grip we held the world !

The orb of Hate had rivers died with blood,
Races in fences held, who dared to steal
By some quaint skill of the mechanic mind
Their rival's sunlight, while their foes, in turn,
Controlled in wallèd impotence the sea,

That they might flood with fear their neighbour's land!
Trade, therefore, in this world of Hate became
Impossible of culture as the wind.
Each mortal lived far from his brother's dreams
And buried deep the product of his mind
From stealing eyes.   Even every father's heart
Was jealous of his child ere it was born !
And then we saw the magic model fade
As though a thought of the Almighty died.
But in this world the spirit of my race
Had no inheritance.

The Orb of Death was strange and wonderful :
It had a tropic beauty.   Luring trees
Held in their branches food for lazy Man ;
No effort of his mind or of his hand
Was needed for his life ; he ate and breathed
And died without a thought of Him who spread
For Man the broad blue deep of Heaven and made
For him the stepping stones of stars.   In ease
And animal delight he passed away
Exalting Death into the crown of Sleep.
This world, too, faded in the ether blue,
As though it floated from the Almighty brain
Into eternal Nothingness.   And here,
Again, the spirit of my race had not
Inheritance !
            Then came the world they named
" Indifference."   An orb like to our own ;
The very birds had not the heart to sing,
The preachers breathed the precepts of the Past :—
" What was, must be ! "   'Twere vain to thrill the
      tongue
With a new song, for none would hear.   No heart
Of revolution pulsed to new-born life ;
There were no drums of discord ; men preferred
To let their valour curdle in their veins.

It was a peaceful world, made for the Day;
They looked not to the Morrow; closed their eyes
To what was looming in the Great Beyond.
They made a monastery of their soul
And built no speculations to the skies!
But this world, too, like to a bubble burst
And left the sky, as though a thought of God
Had come and gone.   And I perceived, again,
That in this world no spirit of my race
Had its Inheritance.
                    But when the orb
Of Love burst on our view our pulses beat
To faster life.   It was God's Treasury
Of Truth for angel eyes, His Book of Man!
Around the orb they gathered as the bees
Flutter to glean their honey and to die.
There read they God as we on earth may read
The strange immortal magic of a man,—
The jewel Thought sparkling in golden Words,—
While in their train foul spirits, gorged with guile,
Came near to breathe their thin vaneering sneers
Made but to hide their wonder!   There I saw
That on no nation did the Almighty scourge
His inharmonious Will, but, in its place,
His Righteousness upon the Masses fell
As dew upon the parchèd blade of grass
Love-longing for its green.   It seemed to me
That each created mind, had, as its boon,
A lens of Righteousness reflecting God,
And every heart had in itself its heaven
(And thus I knew why Shakespeare treasured Truth;
Why the wild soul of Shelley to the lark
Sang its impassioned song, why a calm star
Breeds wonder; why the ocean shouts aloud
Of majesty; why the great sun breathes fear;
Why mountains lift to heaven unmeasured praise;
Why he who scorns moans in a prisoned mind.)

On this fair orb no pitiful poor were seen,
No frozen features starved with cruel cold,
No smoky town hurrying away the green
Scorning to deck its lattices with flowers,
And not a roof was built to hide the stars
Or shut the sun away, for studious Man
Had learnt the lesson in a lens of glass
And had unriddled Nature's chemistry.
And here my race found fair inheritance;
Here Valour flourished in the Court of Love,
And Courage claimed its Palaces of Praise,
And Justice held dominion! And my Guide
With eyes of Glory gazed into my soul
As this thought-kindled world fell through the blue
And plunged into the bosom of our orb!

Then I beheld the watchful angels read
A poem in the little orb of earth,
The author, God, whose very soul had passed
Into the mesmeric entity of Man.

Deem not this blasphemy, diminished mind!
Gaze in the glass of thy being, see thy God;
Blurred, may be, with thine own strange breath of fear,
Forced from thine orthodox mind; but ever there
The Great Communicator stands, whose name,
Longing for lovelier diction, we call,—God;
Who floats in silence o'er the lake of stars,
Who weaves the daisy-carpets of the dell,
Who thrills with feeling every magic nerve,
And canopies our brain with pictured thought,
The All-pervading, Life-inspiring,—God!

As this Thought-Kindled world passed into Man
Lo! there was instant change! For he who held
His finger on his foe with murderous aim
Stayed execution, sought the salient sun,

And gave himself to brotherhood ; no sea
Of rage ere felt so quick a calm.   But I,
And my great Guide, were by a herald borne
From witnessing the earth to a great world
Ten thousand times as large as our loved home
Lit with a dancing, dazzling, amorous light,—
Not flaming like the sun, but like the rays
Of a translucent diamond !   To this
Great scintillating globe in wonder came
From all the island stars within the blue
Unnumbered millions of those happy souls
Who knew the lessons of Mortality.
To them the earth and what they did on earth,
Robed in its dress of Spring, or Winter-clad
In frosty fringe of snow-born icicles,
Was but as boyhood to a Time-taught man,
A pleasant tale to tempt his telling tongue
Or a black memory to hide away.

This mighty world was hollowed of its core,
Like to an orange rifled of its gains,
And in the rind some unpent force had rent
Entrance symmetrical, such as the sea's
Perpetual power caverns through giant rocks.
This vestibule with violet ore and touch
Of rose was stained, and groined with copper's rich
Ebullient hues   And through this wildly wrought
Cathedral cavern we beheld a light,
Rich, red, and radiant as the dying sun :
For in this hollow world a fire still played
In strange fantastic glory round its walls ;
And in the fire all rainbow-hues were seen,
The delicate light of pearls, warm marigold,
Dark violet, lustrous jasmine and deep rose.
Chromatic marvels changing like swift dreams.
And in the vestibule in glory stood
Two spirit Titans of our race, who breathed

Majestic power in gesture, face, and form,
And o'er their heads in spirit-characters
I, with my ether-eyes beholding, read,—
"The Anglo-Saxon Palace of the Soul."
Past these great janitors the spirits flew
Into the mystic orb, ranging their forms
Around the scintillating walls . (for sprites
Have intercourse with fire , behold them flit
Along the electric wires echoing the voice
Of Man, or fashioning the lightning-flash
Flung from obnoxious clouds ') Subtle as thought,
The empty sphere had all its luminous walls
Lined with immortal souls, aglow with zeal,
Aflame with Anglo-Saxon ecstacy

I have seen cherries on a summer tree
Dangling dismay into a child of joy,
But never have I felt such greedy sense
Of what's to come as when this multitude
Saw in the hollow of that burning orb,
Newly admitted from Britannia's throne,
The Saxon Queen Victoria appear !

When her dear body, sundered of her soul,
Passed in a sad procession to its tomb
With muffled drums thudding imperial grief
On her dear London crowd, lo, as a great
Inhabitant of ether, stood the Queen
And Votaress of our Race ; flashed as a thought
From earth to waiting heaven.   She, like the sun,
Dying at Night, had lit another Morn,
Her soul ablush with Righteousness ; her words,
The soft unfoldings of her English tongue.
Making mute captives of our willing ears :—

" Founders and Fathers of the British race,
I come with the passion of earth about me !

My realm, the champion friend of Freedom, stands
Assailed with rancorous riot of untutored tongues,
Wild, tribal tumult of words; as though God,
Who made Mankind, had not made brotherhood,
Or had the Violet taught to slight the Rose !
Our race uprises, like the morn, with glee
And darts derision on these clouds of scorn,
A sweet derision healing as the sun ;
For we shall melt in all and make of all
One people, one great soul, front-faced to Heaven !
In India the rivulet of Love
Runs through the people   In America
Britannia's bond of unity cements
Antagonistic races into one.
('Twas not for naught the *Mayflower* flecked the
    foam.)
The Soul of Man at last triumphant stands
O'er races, tribes, and continents of creeds,
And from our Island comes the Mind
That solves the jealous discords of the world !
For every tongue now learns to lisp our words
Fashioned from all the Babel-lips of Man.
Here stand I, Queen and Empress of my Race,
To prophesy swift glory for mankind :—
The East shall love the West ; the genial South
Shall run with warm embraces to the North ;
The whole mad world shall change ; the American
    States,
Founded and fashioned by free British hearts,
Shall join their proud progenitors, and strike
The bonds of slavery from the wrists of all,
And with the magic of the Free disarm
The world ! Their fleets, united, shall compel
Obedience from the envious, and preserve
The Pride and Dignity of productive Peace.
A man shall be the patriot of the World
Not the perpetual proudling of a people.

And to each heart the golden laws of Christ
Shall with the force of light to all appeal !
The ribbon of Britannia's bond shall tie
Rebellious nations in a knot of Love.
Not Gold, and not Possession, and not Self
Shall rule, but the neighbourly hand that takes
The heart's affection ; and the poor shall grow
Into the soul of the rich, and the child's
Innocence into the mind of a man.
All shall change, and o'er Great Britain's brow
The Lord shall write,—'The Saviour of the World ' "

This was the tender texture of her thought ;
Then the two Titans rent the hollow shell
That had been burning for unnumbered years ;
Slowly it parted like an opening rose,—
The magic millions the encircling leaves
And the great Queen the centre of the flower !—
I saw the Almighty pluck the spirit-bloom
And place it in his bosom, near the heart
Of all creative force : Matter was naught,
Compressible, as Newton's mind had told
In the deep tomes of his " Principia ! "

The end had come, the magic end had come ;
Once more I was a mortal and the bells
Of Christmastide resounded in my ears ;
I heard men's footsteps muffling in the snow.
My Guide slid slowly through the unopened door
And left me with the folios of my words
That I had written as the visions flashed
Their presence o'er the magic of my brain,
And here in volume-form I cast them forth
To claim the kind attention of Man's eyes.

THE END.

POEMS OF IMAGINATION

LOVE IN THE UNIVERSE

REVERIE OF A DOUBTFUL AGNOSTIC

> " Dwells Love not also, then,
>   With Godhead throned on high ?
> This and but this I know :
>   His face I see not there."
>
> WM. WATSON.

O Love ! are these words wise,
True as the lustrous language of the eyes
    And the unconscious words
That nestle in the melodies of birds,
Or are they but a pallid, cold surmise ?

Life, with its fairy Fancy, was to me
    Once as a dreamful apple-blossom spray,
A field of daffodils, a breath of glee,
    The first sweet perfume of the flowers of May ;
In hermitage of violets would I dwell,
My flower-fed soul was hid in each blue-bell.

But now wild thoughts from Evil's fertile fen
Rise like a cloud to blind the minds of men,
        No longer am I gay,
The early sweetness of my world has passed away ;
And though Spring's bridal-blossoms deck her trees

In all my early simple ecstasies,
With murdered innocence I walk through flowers,
And feel soft melancholy touch the hours ;
　　　The veil of this new mind
Clouding my ecstacies bids me be blind !

　　　But why repine ?
In secret sorrow we may grow divine,
　With flowered philosophy we garland grief,
The berries bloom upon the ancient vine,
　　And new, green buds cast off the lingering leaf,
　　　So that my Thought may be
Renewed, though old, and ever, ever free.

　　　Ah ! I would not repine
　　　If that blue heaven were mine,
Once filled by Fancy with ethereal forms
Sublimely silent o'er the breath of storms
　　　Above my flowers sweet,
　A heaven too pure for aught but holy feet ,

With pained perplexity upon my brow
　To this new thought in apathy I bow
And now to me how sacred seems a child
　　With *my* lost breath of glee,
Prattling his fancies, voluble and wild,
　　With *my* first ecstacy !

　　　Ah me ! ah me !
A cultured mind breeds dull philosophy !
I may not see Love's fingers in the sky,
　But only cold-eyed Law ; and dark
　Frowns the wild sea on which I sail my bark,
My only guide, Hope's star,—a petted lie !
I see God gazing down in awful glory,
　　　Cold, Just, and High,
Viewing unfeelingly our human story !

But can I in this blue-domed temple kneeling,
    Question if Love be shown
When I, with simple, reverent feeling,
 Watch the skilled working of that Hand unknown?
The Hand that has through distant æons guided,
    O'er silent realms of space,
Innumerable worlds with giant grace!
(Strange that I hear such wondrous Love derided
Whose every star-world is a loving-kindness,
Each gold-haired sun a miracle to blindness!)

    Ah! surely I can see Love's eye
    Glance from the restless sky
And softly kiss the earth and fretful ocean
    With a manifest emotion?

I place the sunbeam in the hands of Science
And lo! he finds it bid a sweet defiance
To him who sees no Love in hiding there;
    It is the soft abiding place
    Of blooms that blush the maiden's face
    With witchery rare;—
That charm of tender sweetheart maiden
When with her love her bosom is o'er-laden.

Ah! sunbeam, sunbeam! painter of Love's flowers
    In your light, laughing hours,
    Why bid them dance in fertile joy,
    Myriads modest, fair, and coy,
(Like prophets in my new heart stealing,)
If you are not sweet Love with lavish light revealing?

And you, sweet Flowers, why look at me in pity,
And with your pretty scorn laugh down my piteous
    ditty,

116   Love in the Universe

Unless your fragrant breath abroad be flung,
As honied incense from your prophet tongue,
To tell me that your sweets are unavailing
If to my sense they prove not Love unfailing ?

Ye woolly clouds ! that creep along the valleys,
And fall, like cataract, o'er my sight,
Hiding lovely glades and alleys
'Neath your shroud of white,
Are you not the breath of Love
On unseen pinions borne to skies above ?

I see you there, a compact giant soaring,
Tears of tender love outpouring
On the sun-burnt ground ·
Oh ! tender-hearted, tearful comer
Damping down the blaze of summer
With a pleasant sound !

Who bade you, tender, tearful giant,
In the Westward stand defiant,
Like the chivalry of old
Armoured o'er with burnished gold ?
Who made your sunset-hall of rainbow-hues,
Such as we see
Miniatured in morning dews ?
And that pearly, saffron bed
Where the sun's immortal head
May rested be ?
Who bade you wake the Universe in wonder
With your giant thunder
To that great sun ?
Who, but some loving One ?
For in those magic scenes I fain discover
The heart of some Great Lover !

Oh, World ! World ! World !
Would a cold-eyed, stern, Law-giver
Bless us with a silver river
Lovely as a mountain-bride
Wandering through the valleys wide ?
Would he bless the sea with Graces
Sprayed with lovely, creamy laces,
Armed with eyes of deepest blue
Darting tenderest love at you ?
Or is Love his God betraying
When we watch old Ocean playing ?

Ballads from the birds abound :
Would sweet Love forswear their sound ?

And when deep, old Ocean rages,
As do birds against their cages,
Feel you not his breath of salt
Cleanse the deep, blue, airy vault ?
See I not upon his salt breath flying
Sweet, white-winged Love to save weak Life from
    dying ?
Ah ! I know the sailor drinketh
Those salt waves and deathward sinketh,
When old Ocean rises wroth
Leaping at his flying froth ;
And I know the desolation
And the piteous lamentation
Round the shrivelled heels of Famine ;
And I know of floods of waters
Drowning lovely sons and daughters ;
Of the tidal-wave that covers
Many haters, many lovers ;
Of the feverish fire of Death
Burning out our cherished breath ,
And of the earthquake's wide sepulchral jaws
That gape obedient to the Lord of Laws !

I know and see them all :
    I cloak my faith in fear,
And listen, 'till weird whispers fall
    On my enchanted ear ,
Whispers that tell me Love was born
To waft our scattered souls to an Immortal Morn ,
For 'neath the mask of Discord Love lies hid
With melting eye and tender, long-lashed lid,
    Or cruel riddle Life would be
    To our dazed Mortality !

    I float my soul afar
And ask my spirit what these curtains are
    That veil my mind ;—
When lo ! I am enveloped in a dream,
    No longer feel I blind,
Back in an untold æon I behold
    The Earth
Leap as a wild bird from her nest of gold,
And flutter forth upon her starry way
    To seek new birth
In the wide thought of changeful Night and
    Day.
    Behold ! she sees
    Night's diamond mysteries,
Those fairy lamps of God that light the
    blue,—
Worlds that the sun had ever hid from view !
    (E'en as candle-creeds may bury
    Love in Love's own sanctuary)
    But now to her
The dark-eyed Night becomes Interpreter,
    And the great sun grows small,
    A speck of gold in realms celestial !
The breath of God haloes her throbbing orb,
    Envelopes her in blue ethereal,
    Makes her the silver wonder of the Night ;

Trees, plants, and flowers rise to absorb
        God's Life and Light,
And veil her with a garment wrought of rose
    And blue-bell blooms, and lilies white,
      In ever varied, fanciful delight,
'Mid leaves of green that all the flowers enclose.

Thrilled with God's living breath the waters breed
    The tiniest minnow and the giant whale,
And million-mites, like feathered seed,
      Sport their enchanted moment thro' the vale,
    While roaring monsters awe the nightingale !
        Life consumes Life !
    The whole creation seems a beast of prey !
    Look where I will the greater grinds the less
      And then I wonder at her garment gay,
      Her all-pervading loveliness,
'Till Reason rises like a sun-born change
       When glorious Man is born
       Amid the waiting corn,
With boundless Mind o'er granaried wealth to range ;
      For him had grown the flowers,
      The beasts in their green bowers,
The trees, the Universe on which he gazed ;
      I saw Love fall in showers
As Man in silent rapture stood amazed !

        Love ! Love !
     All miracled in thought
watched you lure the earth from that great sun,
    Beheld you light that Primrose of the Sky
      Floating in violet blue ;
To me you are the only Glorious One,
    The mighty motive of the Power on High,
      The one thing true !

120   Love in the Universe

I fling my self-made veil afar,
For while I see a dancing, silver star
     I will not be discourteous to Love's Light,
Or with dull thinking mar
      The magic gleams that break upon my sight!
       Love! as a sea,
With your great soul you are uplifting me!
    Forth from your glory comes a gentle hand,
       It touches me,
      It lifts me into space,
      And thro' the giant Universe I trace
       Fair Beauty's passion
Touching the rose-light of a star, the silver of the
    moon,
And the gold, ardent sunshine of tree-shaded June!
    And that enthralling Beauty, great and free,
    Doth come from you, O Love, uplifting me!

    I am a spirit-mirror, where, behold!
    Pictures more precious than a rose unfold,
      And God pervadeth me;
    No heart has fully to his brother told
    The inner vision his shut eyes behold,
      But none persuadeth me
    That Love is not the Universal Mould
Of God's grand starry dream or Man's poetic thought,
For all sublime creation has by Love been wrought.

LOVE IN THE EARTH

DAINTY Earth is my mother of mirth,
  My delightful elusion, my dream,
My palace of pleasure, my birth
  That reflecteth a far-away gleam.

I would woo her and bid her obey
  Laws of Love penned with pain in her book,
But she, born to her own erring way,
  At fair Wisdom too seldom will look.

I would woo her with tender-told tales,
  She would listen, and sigh, and forget;
And in trouble's delirious gales
  With all her sweet soul she would fret.

That she loves and is loved, is as plain
  As the love of a man and a maid;
That she is not a loss, but a gain,
  The heavens themselves have displayed.

Or why floats she so lightly in heaven
    With her orb of despair?
'Tis by Love she is tenderly driven!
    To Love she is fair!
For she bears the wide Hope of great Man,
    And she builds, like a slave,
For his soul,—a celestial plan,
    For his body,—a grave.
With his intellect, passion, and faith,
    And his wonder at all he may be,
He deems himself only a wraith
    That must flutter and flee;
Only a wraith with a dream,
With an eye of an infinite gleam.

Oh! earth, fold him soft in your breast
  'Tis for him, as a mother, you live,

For your nights and your days know no rest,
  You but live for the love he may give !
God has kissed you with love-lips of fire,
  Kiss Him back, earth, again and again,
Float away with that holy desire
  Leaping up in your bosom of pain
There's a halo around you, sweet orb,
  You are Love in the wonderful sky,
For the soul of great Man doth absorb
  All the love-light poured down from on high.
In the ether you float as a bird,
  It impedes not your wonderful way,
May not conjuring thought then be heard
  When it thinks I may dart as a ray,
As a sprite through that ether to God,
  As the secret, swift lightning will play
Through my mystic, mechanical rod
  With a word, I, to vastness convey

There's an influence flutters and falls
  On my mind each new night and new day,
An emotion that silently calls
  As I gaze at the great starry way :
When I see you, Love, shining there,
  Are you only a beautiful lie ?
Is the thought that encloudeth Despair,
     Love !
A great truth with a terrible sigh ?

Oh, No, No ! I could write from the blue
  With the lightning, and flash to your eyes
My great love, Love, my love true,
  For the *spirit* of Man never lies.

And I am but part of the Earth,
  My delightful elusion, my dream,
My palace of pleasure, my birth,
  That reflecteth a far-away gleam !

TO GOD

BY A NATURE-TAUGHT MODERN

1.

O THOU ! who dost inspire
The mountain-cone with fire,
    Pouring the boiling lava to the plain,
With a new voice
Bid my quick heart rejoice,
    'Till glorious yearnings glow me once again :

2.

That I may utter flames ;
(For this dull mountain shames
    My soaring spirit in the realm of Time ;)
Burn in fire-fear
Earth's thoughts to me too dear,
    And waft me thro' the fire to the sublime

3.

Bear me upon the wings
Of long forgotten things,—
    Of aspirations that have grieved and died,—
And fan my soul,
Till, like a burning coal,
    I breathe myself away in light, and glide

4.

Into great thought of Thee,
Immeasurably free,
    Checked by no boundary that earth may raise,
But sailing wide
Over the wilful tide
    Of human feeling with the breath of Praise,

5.

Let me behold Thy face
And on Thy mountain trace
   The work of Thy feared fingers as I gaze;
Let the fierce flame
Beacon abroad Thy Name,
   That Man's wise eyes may see Thy wizard ways:

6.

For I would touch Thy robe
In this cathedral-globe,
   Where Thou art shrined in mystic Night and Day,
And I would crave
A heart made strong and brave
   To break earth's God of superstitious clay:

7.

To watch a star in space
And through its orbit trace
   Thy geometric finger in the blue;
To feel Thy thought
In Thy fair flowers inwrought
   Preaching sweet sermons to the listening few;

8.

To see Thy quiet eye
In the pervading sky
   And know Thou art the Secret of the dead;
To list in fear
With strange, prophetic ear
   To all the Wisdom that has breathed and fled,

9.

To see Thy light shine down
Upon Man's complex town,
   Ripening the thoughts of thousands 'til they yield

Fruit like Thy trees'
Delicious ministries,—
   Delicate wonders ever unrevealed;

10.

To smell Thine incense, Lord,
Wafted in love abroad,
   Upon the breath of roses and of pines;
To taste in glee,
With a sweet thought of Thee,
   The trampled essence of the juicy vines!

11

But O, my God! Content
Blackens Thy firmament,
   Blots out Thy mount of fire, destroys my zeal,
Until I lie
In opiate apathy,
   Gaze in Thine eyes of Love and cannot feel!

12.

Therefore Thy touch of Pain
Doth prove a pleasant gain,
   And goads me to Endeavour thro' Despair;
In quickened Guilt
I feel the jewelled hilt
   Of that keen sword that kills what's falsely fair.

13.

O, wrap me round and round,
Wake me with magic sound,
   Pour Heaven's grand harmonies into mine ears,
Let Hope's lute play
Upon my soul all day.
   'Till I complete my symphony of years!

14.

Give me deep sense of Thee,
A sweet divinity
    To make Life sacred tho' I walk in pain ;
To know each thought
Is in Thy presence wrought,
    Tho' forged in the hot furnace of my brain !

15.

Let not my soul pass by
The world's majestic sigh
    And with cold heart forget, like hermit lone,
My brother's woe,
Feeling it beat more slow
    When with accustomed ear I hear him groan

16.

Forgive these jaded cries
Lord of my mysteries !
    In whose kind Hand I see the ripening peach
Sunning its soul ;
I, like a hidden mole,
    Burrow in earth and scorn what thought doth teach !

17.

I know ! I know ! I know !
That is the silent blow
    Secretly knocking at my yearning heart,
And yet I dare
Scoff at Thy listening air
    And dream my soul may play a double part !

18.

O God ! Thou Great Unknown !
Thou Thought 'mid blossoms blown,
    Thou strange, outspreading Spirit in the blue.

Thou Dream of earth,
Thou Passion of my birth,
  Thou Mighty Eye lighting my Nature thro' !

19.

Teach me the task of Death,
The truth that Nature saith,
  The lesson-moments of my careless days
When I have heard
The spirit-spoken word,
  'Mid glimpse of wonder thro' the uplifted haze,

20.

When the enraptured bird
Has the hushed woodland stirred
  With overflowings melodied in praise !
So that I may
In Thee view each new day,
  With eyes endowed with rich, expectant gaze.

21

And the dull world may roll
Round my magnetic soul
  While I draw new, ripe wisdom from Thy rays,
And die at length
Full of receptive strength,
  Ready to roam in Thy unbounded ways !

TO GOD

BY A CULTURE-KILLED MODERN

I.

God! who didst love the Jew,
Who wondrous pictures drew
   Of Thy just, merciful, but awful sway;
Wilt Thou love me,
So modern and so free,
   Too proud to own a Maker, or to pray?

2.

Too proud? Nay: not too proud!
I am but as yon cloud,
   Born but to live, and move, and melt in air;
The earth that blooms
Its flowers, itself consumes,
   How can it then rejoice that I am fair?

3.

That I think Thee divine
Is no false thought of mine,
   It is my simple father's dream of Thee;
And in his name
I strive to fan the flame
   Which once lit up his strange Idolatry.

4.

Lord, then, (if Thou be Lord,)
Prepare Thy spirit-sword,
   And all the armoury that makes Thee strong;
And flash on me
Some wondrous thought of Thee,
   Some miracle to wake me into song!

5.

My baby comes to me
And presses prettily
   His tiny hands, and, smiling, says Thee prayers;

His prattle done
He sleeps until the sun
Brings him new playthings, new delights, and cares.

6.

Would I could pray, in fear,
As he into Thine ear;
Then should I feel that Life is still a joy:
To feel forgot
Is my unhappy lot,
I envy much my trustful baby boy.

GOD—A CHILD'S SONG

THE air, it is the breath of God,
The sun, it is His eye,
The stars, the magic jewels
Wrought in His robe of sky;

The mountains are His steps to heaven,
The valleys are His dream,
Where roses bloom, and violets hide,
And fishes stem the stream;

The trees are where His worshippers
Amid green leaves will sing
Immortal music to the Morn
That brings the flower-clad Spring.

So *great* is He that in the night
I see His hand afar
Moving amid the heavenly host
The most majestic Star:

So *small* is He that in my heart
I can both see and hear
His spirit-form, His magic voice,
Unconscious of a fear.

I

NATURE'S SONG

THERE's a song in the heart of a man
　　That will ring in the heart of the world,
　　　　If it mingle true
　　　　With the green and the blue
　　And the song that the brooklet has purled;

If it come like the nightingale's note
　　To the heart of the listening night,
　　　　Or like breath of a maid
　　　　When her heart's afraid
　　Lest the love of her lover be light;

If it only be true-love to Truth
　　And will sing with emotional breath,
　　　　To the lips it will rise
　　　　Like a lark to the skies,
　　And live on all unconscious of Death.

WINTER'S COME!

1.

WINTER's come!　Can you not hear him
　　Creeping round now all is dark?
　　　　Moaning, wailing
　　　　As though ailing;
　　Hoarse of voice; and hark!

2.

Sound not his rough plainings louder
　　Than they sounded yester e'en?
　　　　Sighing, crying,
　　　　Onward flying,
　　Tearing through the green.

3.

Tossing leaves in aimless fury
  'Gainst the happy, home-lit pane,
    All his bluster
    Makes us muster
Round the hearth again.

4.

We will not admit this brawler
  With his hard, cold, callous air ,
    Come and shelter
    From this pelter
Of the leaves of Care.

5.

We have pressed the grapes of Summer
  And have stored the laughing wine ,
    Let the lasses
    Fill the glasses,
And in dance divine,

6.

Step to dainty strains of music
  Ministered by flute and string,
    'Till the hours
    Bring the flowers
And the songs of Spring.

MY SOUL

1.

I HAVE wandered through life with my soul
   And touched the hem of uncleanness,
Though flowers have leapt to my lips
And yielded me Life's honey sips
   Yet slave-born am I to my meanness.

2.

In my bosom I treasured my gold
   Tarnished with touch of slavery,
But a maid's lily finger-tips
Stole the gold as she kissed my lips
   And slave am I to her knavery.

3.

I could laugh at my ignorant soul,
   Laugh at my own delusion,
But there comes a great fear in the night
When some terror creeps forth with a light,
   And my laugh dies away in confusion.

4

I could go to a priest with my soul
   And crave his holy blessing,
But a silent something seems to say :—
"Turn soul and wash thy stains away,
   Is there virtue in such confessing?"

5.

What hast thou done with my dreams, O soul!
   That sang like birds to thy morning?
Are they dead beneath a dewless sky
Where the seed of thought is sown to die
   With never a blossom adorning?

6.

I have locked my fair dreams in their cage
 And forth have gone a-roaming ;
But I've heard their little fluttering wings
Seeking me 'mid unholy things
 While the steed of Time stood foaming.

7.

With the treacherous breeze of the world
 My soul flirts as a feather,
Raised without reason, downward cast,
Then hurried onward by the blast ;—
 E'en Freedom may sigh for a tether !

8.

I have watched a great soul beat the air
 With the wings of his ambition,
But as he flew his vision fair
Became enclouded in Despair
 And the world's eyes glanced derision !

9.

I can gather but scorn for my soul
 For I have joined the scorning ;
The curling lip I oft have curled,
Sneering with the sneering world,
 Truth's finger uplifted in warning !

10.

O, the scorner knows naught of his joy
 Who dares the flight and faileth :
The envious soul disdains his peer
And puffs his prideful, paltry sneer,
 But the sneer of none availeth !

11.

'Tis for gold that the soul of man craves,
    The gold that owns no master ;
It is as friendly to my hand
As to the highest in the land,
    But lureth us all to disaster !

12.

I have kissed in dreams the lips of love,
    Kissed, and my soul has lingered,
But never have I seen Love's tear
Smooth away the worldly sneer
    While the dust of the gold was fingered.

13

Ah ! if I did not moated stand,
    Fortressed against my brother,
Might I not then be led a slave,
Tortured by a wilier knave
    Who would capture the soul of another ?

14

And so I hail these mortised bones,
    This flesh that owns me keeper,
These eyes that show but half my soul
And cunning, in their sockets roll
    As a laugher or as a weeper !

15.

Buried am I in my flesh and bones,
    Pricked by the needle of feeling ;
I am an untranslated book
To my brother's prying look ;
    I might be Hypocrisy kneeling,

16.

Or the cathedral's holiest soul
  For aught he could discover;
I might be angel, god, or man,
A devil to his every plan,
  Or the shrine of his unknown lover!

17.

There's a hush in the depths of my soul,
  E'en when the lips are speaking,
I might be myriad leagues away
From the delusions of the day
  While the Source of Thought I am seeking!

18.

And I pour out my Thought as a flood
  That falls into the ocean,
The melting vowels leap and chase
Each other with a liquid grace
  And a sweet, melodious motion: .

19.

Yea, these boiling waves of my brain
  Leap forth with loud explosion
From the moving ledge of my tongue,
As the cataract waves are flung
  On the rocks in rapid erosion.

20.

They seem to come from regions strange
  To this round world of Matter,
From lips of Love that sing afar
Beyond the Light-created star
  And with no false words do they flatter.

21.

As they pass through my receptive brain
  I think in sun and showers,
In holy-hearted joy or pain,
In love that never can be slain,
  And in lovelier dreams than flowers;

22.

For I see a Light surpassing sense
  Of eyes that smile on roses,
A light that lights a palace fair
Without foundations in the air
  Where the Spirit of Truth reposes!

23.

I might be borne on the wings of Speed
  The flight of Light exceeding!
Where is the plummet of my soul
And where its ever moving goal?
  I walk the flowered earth without heeding:

24.

For my soul spends its days as a dream
  Lost in a Babel of thinking:
Yet round me lies that Silence deep
Like a giant laid asleep
  From whose waking each hour I seem shrinking.

25.

O thou silent, immutable Sense
  Enveloping my being,
Ye seem an eye outside of me
To aid my mighty soul to see
  What the spirits beyond are seeing!

26.

And I feel the burden of a frown
  When the Sense 'gainst me is moving,
Piercing me as with a spear
By Conscience made with hands of fear
  But I joy in that Sense's approving.

27.

O thou silent Deep, thou silent Deep !
  In which my soul seems breathing,
As I play with earth for a day,
And I look, and laugh, and am gay,
  Thou art mysteries round me wreathing !

28.

Dost thou say to me, thou who art rich,
  Thou who art dainty in raiment,
That the standard of Life is gold,
That virtue is purchased and sold,
  That innocence smiles but for payment ?

29.

O thou rich ! when Time clads thy proud bones
  With saintly crape of sorrow,
Canst thou bribe with thy gold the tear,
Or bid anguish disappear,
  Or command thee a happy to-morrow?

30.

Thou wilt yearn for the sweet vanished love
  Hid in the dim Hereafter :
And though ye may carelessly walk
And callously humour thy talk
  There is pathos born in thy laughter !

31.

A sweet pathos thy soul cannot drown
 In shallow worldly waters,
For the agonized heart must grieve
O'er the spirits that silently leave
 But the bodies of sons and daughters.

32.

Oh, thy Gold may be flung in the grave
 As worthless dung of Matter :
It may yield thee a libertine son
A daughter with heart undone,
 And the glory of life it may shatter !

33.

But why yearn for the sight of the lost
 If yearning dies in yearning?
Does fair Nature scoff at my side
When Hope, my brilliant bride,
 The lantern of ecstacy burning,

34.

Walks with my soul to the grave of fear
 And conjures up a vision
Of greetings in a holier clime
Beneath the smile of the Sublime
 When the rose of Life reaps fruition?

35.

For it cannot be that we behold
 Our love in fleshly casement
And melt our being in her soul
Only to find the grave our goal
 And in dust of the earth effacement.

36.

Flinging this thought that our soul denies
  Upon earth's funeral altar
We shall fly away on tongues of fire
Higher, higher, ever higher
  When th' automaton heart doth falter.

37.

I have glanced in the Book of the Dead
  And seen my own name entered
And I have wept to see it there
Until I felt my spirit fair
  With its eyes on a new life centred.

38.

I have seen a loom weave threads of gold
  To patterns of perfection ,
So with the shuttle of the earth
Our God designs our spirit-birth
  Say the sunken eyes of Reflection.

39.

And He cares if we come or we go,
  Or if our hopes enraptured
Great palaces of Thought uprear,
Where all delusions disappear,
  Or if snared by earth we are captured.

40.

Light me a torch at the brink of Hell
  That I may show my neighbours
The darkened side of wondrous Truth,
The perilous pathway of our youth
  Through the flashing of Evil's sabres.

41.

Does a God of emoluments cry :—
"Come to my heart, ye Winner !
Ye have filched your brother's gold
Ye are callous, wise, and bold,
    I delight in the soul of a sinner ? "

42.

Yet 'twas thus I went down to the sea
    And launched my soul in glory,
And thundered cannon far and near
At him who deigned to be my peer ;
    Ah ! I utter in shame my story.

43.

And I carried my soul to the wars,
    And blew a shrill defiance
With the bugle played by my tongue,
And to death my foes were flung
    By the dynamite hand of Science.

44

But the Hate that uprose with that blast
    Died when the soul grew wiser ;
And I asked my rude Reason why
I blew that bugle's battle cry
    And became my own soul's despiser ?

45.

I have gone with my soul to the dance
    And tasted cups of pleasure,
With the Violet I was sad,
With the Lily I was glad,
    With the Rose-bud I danced full measure.

46.

Yet they said it was vain to be lured
　By touch of dainty maiden
By the lips that whisper Truth
In the quickened ear of youth
　With Life's new philosophy laden !

47.

So I crushed in my fingers the flowers
　That round my soul were playing,
I hid like a monk in a cave
And spurned the sweet gifts that Life gave :
　Nature passed me with lips and hands praying.

48.

Praying loud for a soul that was dead
　To Nature's tender teaching,
So I rose like a spring-born flower
In a laughing sunny hour
　With a look of sweet love, beseeching.

49.

I have said to the Master of Science :—
　" Thou who art great truths gleaning,
Canst thou measure my soul with a rod,
Or deny me my unseen God,
　Or divine my mystical meaning ? "

50.

And the new sage of Science has said :—
　" Behold ! thou art some wonder,
I cannot weigh or measure thee,
To Matter thou art mystery,
　Thou art greater than sun-made thunder ! "

51.

Once I opened the lips of my soul
   With some new Vision burning.
But as I thought not with the crowd
They spurned the words I said aloud,
   Not a ghost of my thought discerning.

52.

I was cut by the wind of their scorn,
   They rose as one to battle,
Around me leapt the martyr's flame,
I saw the stake, I felt the shame;
   They were brutal as herds of cattle.

53.

But a quiet was hid in my soul,
   I felt in some Great Presence
That seemed to make the great Thought flame
Until it burnt my solid frame
   To a living, strange incandescence.

54.

And the earth slowly measured the years
   While souls of men were growing,
And then I saw my Vision come
With herald, trump, and beat of drum,
   The world its new homage bestowing.

55.

Though the world to me was growing gray,
   The life-light in me fading,
They bore me in their buoyant arms,
Shouted my name and praised my charms
   With a flattery most degrading

56.

Too late, alas ! for I saw afar
  A lovelier Truth appearing,
And trooping with it gentler feet,
And wiser heads with words more sweet,
  No roar of brutality fearing.

57.

So I say to my wonderful soul —
  " I find thee ever changing,
I knew thee not an hour ago,
Ye bloom not as the blossoms blow,
  Like a bee ye are ever ranging.

58.

" And a magical vision is thine
  That seems for aye expanding,
Out-stepping the swift feet of Light
Farther than ken of human sight,
  Though on earth in impotence standing."

59.

So my magic spirit joys to be
  A thought expanding ever ;
It is no owner of a grave,
Or to my body bound a slave,
  Such a mortal conception—never !

60.

Thus to the grave with my soul I went
  And said to the Dust-bearers .—
" Toss in my body if ye will
And with the mournful music thrill
  Thy Flesh of which still ye are wearers."

61.

Then have they questioned each other's eyes
  Each at my whisper wondering,
And at night their bones have knelt to pray
Fear-picturing their own grave-day
  With the sunset clouds far thundering.

62.

If I leave the light-house of my eyes
  Who can illume the lenses?
A mist is on the mirror blurred,
No ray of light is flashed and stirred,
  Dead are the passionate frenzies.

63.

I have questioned the light of my eyes
  And catechized my hearing,
Asked all my senses if they know
Him who rules them here below?
  They have answered with lips despairing!

64.

Can an instrument play me a tune,
  Can it ravish me with laughter,
Or dissolve in tears of woe
Or in sunny Hope-buds blow
  Or dream of a Here and Hereafter?

65.

I have gone on a morning of May
  With the sun upon the mountains,
And the dew in Nature's hand
Scattering diamonds o'er the land
  While the rainbows laughed in the fountains ;

66.

While the vales were rapturous with flowers,
  Light-hearted birds a-singing
Tumultuous music from their throats,
In a thousand happy notes,
  But to me no joy were they bringing,

67.

For I seemed afloat upon a sea
  Of endless waves of thinking
That were not of my flesh-veins born,
They took no notice of the morn
  As though earth in a mist were sinking.

68.

And I was left in the sea of blue
  On God's thought-ocean sailing,
Like some lone star, with not a sound
Breaking the depths of the profound ;
  My thought o'er my body prevailing.

69.

So if I may part myself from earth
  While the magic heart is beating,
May not I scorn garrotter Death,
Slinking behind to choke my breath
  While I look for the heavenly greeting ?

70.

I have plunged into Omar's mind
  And felt my Being falling
Into a pessimistic sea
Where never life of man may be,
  Where the syren of Death is calling.

K

71.

And my soul has arisen like flames
  From the enfolding billow
And burnt with irony of hate
Omar's book of dismal Fate
  That he wrote on his nightmare-pillow.

72.

Not that my magical soul derides
  The great delight of being,
The life that in the footstep lives,
The boundless ecstasy that gives
  My soul the conception of fleeing.

73.

My heart responds to the bard of earth
  Who lives 'mid flowers and grasses,
Laughs with the sun and weeps with the rain,
And hides with blooms the grave of pain,
  And sports with the kiss of the lasses

74

Yea, my soul delights in mortal joy,
  I am no hermit hiding,
Shutting my spirit in a cell
From sound of bridal or burial bell
  In selfish delusion abiding.

75.

Like a bee I suck the Rose of Hope
  And Life's pure honey treasure,
And toil with firm Ambition's hand
That I may move o'er sea and land
  With the sunny delight of pleasure.

76.

Who can gather my life when I die,
  Capture the charm of my being,
Point to a vanishing drop and say,
"That is the essence of the clay,
  The Life that inspired the seeing?"

77.

And if none may find it, then, I trow,
  It must escape our vision,
It cannot like a log lie dead
Silent in a leaden bed,
  That spirit that knoweth derision.

78.

Mightier than roar of the thunder
  Forging the daggers of heaven
Is the flashing presence pent
In this fertile tenement,
  This house for a time to me given.

79.

For my soul the wild lightning can turn
  To a message for my brother,
Can trace God's universal laws,
And, like a lion, 'tween its paws
  Can play with the soul of another.

THE SCEPTIC VEIL

I saw a cloud fall on the minds of men,
 A strange dull cloud
Raised by old Evil from his stagnant fen ;
It hid not sun or moon from mortal ken
 But like a shroud
It seemed to quench Man's inner sense of Light
And men, like owls, gazed only at the Night !

Some said 'twas wondrous ; but my soul saw naught
But dull, infectious, strange disease of Thought,
That bade men wrap their minds in shrouds of gray
As though they would obliterate the Day :
 But I was young ;
I seemed to have no bridle to my tongue,
And from my eyes the cloak of cloud I flung
And wandered everywhere with heart of glee,
 Free, free, tumultuously free !
 The centuries for me had writ their Word,
 A word that no new hand could teaze away ;
 It spoke as freely as a tuneful bird
 Lilts to the woodlands his love-laden lay :
  And the Word said,
  Bowing his Wisdom head :—
" I, Heart of Man, have strived through million-eyes
To pierce the veil of Life's deep mysteries ;
 Hope has before my gaze
 Danced in a thousand ways,
But Love has lilted to me one true song,
And though I see but little, yet I long
For something higher, something more than I
Can find embosomed in the earth or sky."

THE FUTURE LIFE

1.

Living, loving, I have longed
  For the greater life to come.
Though my years my soul have wronged,
  Though my tongue with age be dumb,
Yet the dream can never die
That illumes the inner eye.

2.

Lo! I see the picture plain
  That the artist-years have wrought
On the canvas of my brain
  With the brush of centuried thought
Dipped in colours Nature-made
To the finest rainbow-shade.

3.

Though I be a beggar born
  I can paint my picture fair
With the colours of the Morn
  Glowing on the brush of care;
Neither Title, Power, nor Place
Mould for God the spirit-race.

4.

I my future seem to weave
  With the brain's rebellious threads;
I can but myself receive;
  Man each day his future weds;
As I break through Death's dark door
My wrought future looms before.

5.

What I live for, that I gain;
  Silently the end is won,
Though the victory be not plain
  'Neath the warm, material sun;
Thus the spirit-bud shall bloom
In the Light beyond the tomb.

TO A LILY OF THE VALLEY

CAN I ever understand,
  Lily! with the fragrant breath!
Life that passes through the land?
  Tell me, Lily—life-in-death!

I have read the Sacred Page,
  I have felt Man's breath go by,
Suffered from his blistering rage
  And his vast eternal sigh.

But I have not heard him say
  What impelled him in his youth,
For, alas, when he is gray,
  Frosted lips evade the truth!

I am but a lily living
  In the laughter of the sun,
I am ever lessons giving
  To the sweet observant one;

And to you I will unfold
  All the passion of my being,
As a sunny beam of gold
  Brings to all the joy of seeing :—

Man has come to me and sighed
  That he was not as a flower,
That he must be crucified
  Ere he finds his happy hour.

He has wondered at my joy,
  Naked in the golden sun,
Even to his thoughtless boy
  I am as a wondrous one.

He with all his eyes alight
   Studies my fantastic bells,
And the wonder of the sight
   All his dull despair dispels.

For, he says, he cannot see
   Hidden in the unconscious earth
Anything that patterned me
   Into measured bells of mirth

Never was a flower evolved
   From a laughing, sunny beam,
Never was a lily solved
   By a dull, Darwinian dream.

THE LIGHT OF DEATH

A BEREAVED ONE'S COMMUNION WITH HER HEART

1.

SPRINKLE no flowers upon his grave,
   No dying flowers,
  But let the light of lilies blow
  Radiant from his heart below,
As though he still sweet virtue gave,
   As in Life's hours,
Breathing the innocence of lily-flowers.

2.

I would not bid thee utter groans
   Now he has fled,
  But I would tell enquiring ears
  His absence brings me no new fears,
For he resides not with his bones ;
   Where he lies dead
Some new-born light is mystically shed.

3.

O ! well I know, if he appeared,
      Soft peach-like bloom
Would hurry to my faded face,
And I, apparelled in new grace,
Would move in all he loved and feared ;
      Life would illume
With his pure lily-light my soul of gloom

4

But now my eyes in fear have seen
      The light that came
When he, endeared by nature's charms,
Slid coldly through my nursing arms
And left a trailing meteor sheen
      Of rose-white flame
Across my darkness while I sobbed his name.

5.

And if he came 'twould not be well :
      You, Heart ! and I
Would deem him but a thing untrue,
For he has fled beyond the blue,
Beyond our human heaven and hell,
      And now knows why
No form dare enter earth again to die.

6.

If his fond form came back to bloom
      And fade away,
We then should know that Hope had fled
From the charmed regions of the dead,
And came before the frozen tomb
      Again to play
His ancient beckonings from day to day.

7.

Death kindly touched my weary eyes
      And bade me see
  The spirit-pageant in the air
  Smiling at our divine despair ;
Revealed their whispered thought, so wise,
      So good, so free,
And now I live with them, and they with me.

8.

All the fine feelings of my brain
      Seem to respond
  To some life-giving Sense unseen,
  But present in the blue and green,
In kiss of sun and tears of rain ;
      Some love-made bond
Binds me to that deep Sense, Here and Beyond.

9.

Thus Death has shed into my soul
      A lovelier light
  Than Life with all its blue ablaze
  Sunned on the summit of its days !
And round me lovelier regions roll
      Than my dull sight
Can glean through bluest lenses of the night !

10.

Therefore from these fine memories I
      Can never part ,
  Not for all treasures earth may bring,
  Though jewelled with her dew-gemmed Spring,
Would I Death's fairy threads untie ;
      There is no mart
Where Love may sell thy memories, O my heart !

THIS CROWN OF THORNS

THIS crown of thorns! Must I bear it
   Crushed on my brow in pain?
May not another wear it?
   Would it be all in vain
To curse with curling lips and burst
   The sad, strong, heavy chain
That binds me to my conscience curst?
   Would it be all in vain?

Great Love! I must endure unshaken
   All pain, all sense of fear,
For I can hear wise spirits waken
   Weird music in my ear,
Memorial music from the tongue
   Of prophet and of bard
Who to the deafened millions sung,
   Rough stones their strange reward!

EMOTION, WRITTEN AND SPOKEN

THE studied word, the polished phrase,
   The published utterance brings delight,
But ah! as on the print I gaze
   Oft doubt I if I read aright.

But when I see the flashing eye,—
   The lightning quivering from the heart,—
For no interpreter I cry,
   The revelation needs no art,

The lips spring into wordy flood,
   In vapourous shroud they seem to flow
Like cataracts coursing through my blood:—
   And then I wish I did not know.

TO MY BROTHER

ON OUR MOTHER'S DEATH

October 15th, 1900

I.

LIKE sweet light she has departed,
　Brother, bid them toll the bell,
That we two may, broken-hearted,
　Sound our sorrow thro' the knell;
The Awful tone may scare the gloom
And break the dumbness of the tomb.

But the silence is unbroken,
　Not a conscious human ear
Hears a fairy whisper spoken
　From the still lips on the bier;
Not a wind that passes by
Brings a rumour of her sigh.

Touch dull Death's dark curtain, brother,
　Press it, feel; she is behind;
That loved presence of our mother
　Through her gray eyes looking kind,
Lo, they burn their silent tale
Through the dark and sullen veil.

Something lifts the curtain, brother;
　'Tis a gust of spirit-air
Wafted by our gentle mother,
　And I see her standing there,
Not a tender tear I trace
Flooding woe down her loved face.

Bid them hush that tolling, brother,
　Dry the tear-drops in that bell,
This communion with our mother
　Finds no language in a knell,

Gently in our heart she glides
And as spirit-guest resides.

2.

She has left us, brother, sighing,
   Heaven's new light upon her face,
None can surely call it dying
   Thus to flit with such mute grace.

I believe that Death, while dreaming,
   Took her for a winter-rose,
Then awoke, and found her gleaming
   In the Bosom of Repose

3

Her soul has passed beyond our dream,
   Beyond our furrowed human thought,
Like a fair fisher by a stream
   She has been in the torrent caught
And swept afar from faces dear
Into the marble sea of fear.

The pleasant laughter in her eyes,
   The hands that touched away our pain
Have gone, and yet to my surprise
   They seem to visit us again,
In the wide mansion of our heart
She still performs a mother's part.

Let not cold Science rise and say
   These are but fancies in the blood
And sweep these blessed thoughts away
   Into his dull material flood ;
Stars are but stones ! the soul is free
To flit into Immensity

THE NEW-BORN CENTURY

I FEEL some magic finger touch my arm
And lead me to the new-born Century
Cradled in Light!   His little hand extends,
He greets me; lisps his little words; his eyes,
Far gleaming down the dust of years, alive
To all the portents that pervade his birth,
Smile inward recognition.   As a babe
He pushes back the Past; he laughs and cries
At all the wonders that press on his view;
He takes the toy of Earth and spins it round,
He laughs at stars and all the sons of stars,
Laughs at the crazy millions to be born
With whom his hands will play; laughs at the dreams
That old men bring to him,—at musty thought,
Fruit of decaying brains;—for he sees *Light*
And knows that he must follow, whether bard
Sing songs of wild rebellion or of joy:
His baby-limbs must stumble after Light,
It is his golden Kingdom.   Not a gem
Will lure him like a lamp when eve grows dark
Around the windows of his mind; not a toy
Brings him the silent value of sweet Light;
He would embrace it with both hands and sear
His baby-fingers!   He would lave in it
As in a lake translucent of fine gold.
At his feet the tapestry of Peace they spread;
It is his playground where his soldiers toy
With immemorial War; and if you dare
With these vain, pretty troops refuse him play
He will but rave, for he pretends to sleep,
Cradled and fended by these toys of War.
Pretends to sleep, for if you do but touch
His cherished Honour he upgirds to slay!
(He still holds Honour 'neath his plated shield

158 Beauty in Loving-Kindness

As a weird, hidden treasure none may soil,
But in full time Honour shall fended be
By the soft, tender pleading of Love's eyes.)
Pricked with his playful fingers bubbles break
About his baby-mind ; and he prepares
To make salubrious war on feeble thought
That leads not where Light dazzles. Bring him Maps
And every demarcating line will he
Smudge with his baby finger, for he laughs
At Kingdoms and the pride of Kings, and moves
The millions 'till the races blend like streams,
And none can trace their interlacing bands
In love-knots bound. Give him Books ; and he
Will choose one language for all tongues that none
May strangers be, eyeing each other's lips
With mute suspicion. Give him Science grave ;
And he will with each tender nerve of Thought
Abstract the truth and make man's Bible big
With God's own word. Then give him Pen ; and he
Will write the love-born lay of unity
And with a sweet contention gently charm
New pages to a hundred years of life.
The world seems trembling into eloquence,
And when the graves have closed above our bones
His mightier son shall edit with his pen
The next great Century of mortal thought,
And onward through the ages men shall read
The living journal of each century !

BEAUTY IN LOVING-KINDNESS

I HAVE tried to touch the sky,
To peer into a maiden's eye,
But, alas, a cloud has caught
All the efforts of my thought ;
In a mist the love-lights die
Like the starry eyes on high.

Beauty comes to me like death,
Cold and senseless is her breath,
I can never make her feel
Half the love that I conceal,
Half the cravings, half the fears,
Half the joys blown down the years.

I would cast a star away,
To a jewel I would say :—
" Banish all your Beauty far
Nothing lives in gem or star,
Only lovely life I find
In a human heart that's kind."

A TRIBUTE
TO THE REV. DR MOMERIE

UPON WHOSE LIGHT THE ORTHODOX PLANTED
THE BUSHEL

Written on the day after his sudden death

1.

THERE was a gentle raid on earth last night
   When jealous angels dropped into our gloom
And bore our great belovèd from our sight,
   Leaving his books to light his silent room ;
They were a brilliant band, by Love made gay,
They smiled on him as sunbeams on the may,
Till like a flower he turned his soul to Light,
And left his body for ethereal flight !

2.

We dare not envy them their precious prey ;
   The creed-crammed world would not by him be fed,
Would never soar into his eagle-way,
   And would not be by his loved logic led ;

160 Tribute to the Rev. Dr Momerie

Therefore in tears he argued through his pen,
And wrote the message of his mind to men,
His sun-clear mind,—a god of thought at play,—
Through all his work shedding religious day.

3

If we had held him with magnetic eyes
　Or claimed his eloquence with myriad ears
He might not then have been the angels' prize
　Passing so suddenly into our tears ;
Such love had lured his lips to fine excess
Clothing great joy in verbal loveliness,
And then the silent sorrow in his gaze
Had not rebuked the world's unkindly ways.

4.

How oft are priests our tender Lord's despair !
　If Christ breathed with us now would He refuse
To purge from blasphemy our books of prayer,
　To cull from Science all its rose-bud news
And watch its fair unfoldings, freeing eyes,
And ears and tongue from smothering mask of lies ?
Yet for these things the prelates of God's lore
Shut 'gainst this martyred mind their sacred door !

5.

My minister ! my gentle minister !
　Still will your presence preach perpetual prayer,
Still will you be God's true interpreter,
　And still with you in each drawn breath of air
I'll feel for God over the star-lit blue
And search the buried Past for treasures true ;
In me for ever is your soul astir,
My minister ! my gentle minister !

SAINT PAUL'S

I WAS drawn by the Spirit of Prayer
  To the great cathedral dome,
To breathe through the yearning air
  My heart to my Unknown Home,
    Where? ah where?
It is not in the brain of a man to tell
Though he inwardly feel the magic spell!

I heard the priest with a measured grace
  Chant magical prayers,
And I felt I was looking my God in the face.

  As an angel unawares
May glide into the realms of space
  And feel interminable fear
  Away from all his fellows dear,
  Away from all his angel cares,
    So felt I there!

  On the walls there were flags
    Tattered by breezes of glory,
  Tattered to eloquent rags
    Telling a soldier-story,
Telling of deeds that were done
In the sleeping night or the wakeful sun
By the venturesome men who gave
Their souls to the God of the Grave!

Around me were moving vast millions
  Unconscious of God or of me,
And the stars were careering in trillions
  In the depths of the ether-sea;

In the cellular realms of my brain
  My God was enthroned,
I felt His beneficent reign
  And His wisdom I owned;
I was calmed in the storm of the earth,
I was charmed into magical birth.

I rose on the pinions of prayer
Into the yielding air,
And the fabric upward flew
With my soul into the blue,
All the worshippers and choir
Floated with my soul's desire,
Till the sound of the great cathedral bell
On the ears of the listening angels fell

The angels fluttered through every wall,
  The stones great streams of light became,
And I heard those dull materials fall
  Again to earth in dust and shame;
  The mighty pile, the dome of Fame,
  Changed to a tenement of flame.
'Twas strange to see those walls grow bright,
  The statues flutter into fire,
The very altar turn to light,
  The contour kept from base to spire,
  The bodies dull that with me flew
  Blaze into spirits that I knew!

As sunbeams in a diamond shine
  Those souls reflected some great Sun,
And then I knew I was divine,
  The miracle of life begun,
The angels crowded round the dome,
  The magic dome of restless fire;
That dome of fire became my home,
  In every flame I fluttered higher.

The angels read me as I read
Imaginations built by man
In paper-palaces of words,
I knew at last that I was freed
From man's cold fixity of plan
That knows no freedom as of birds;
I was emancipated quite
From death and darkness into light!

And the Spirit through the blazing walls
Came as the sun in Spring
Flings diamonds in the waterfalls,
Buds hope in everything;
I felt the feelings of a tree
When from the clinch of Winter free.

And to that Spirit I was drawn
As fountains fascinate a fawn,
As stars through my rapt eyes at night
Draw forth my being in delight
And to my senses whisper clear
The secrets of each moving sphere.

I seemed to lift the Earth to Heaven
And kneel upon it to the Lord,
And then the dome of Heaven was riven
With Love's weird universal chord,
And as it through my heart-strings ran
I sang the melody of Man,
And bore in prayer the human cry
Into the Vestibule on High.

THE SPELL

AN ALLEGORY

I.

No sound was heard
Save the fret of a bird
Fluttering his wings in fear,
As Death passed by
With his measured sigh
And his masquerading bier;
Silently passed he with hearse and pall
And the dark sleek feathers that flatter us all.
I looked from my window and drank in deep
The mournful pageant that makes us weep.

2.

The moon shone cold
And I was bold
To question the scene I saw,
So I raised the window and felt with fear
The soul of the body that passed on the bier
Slip into my own
With a shudder and groan
(And the bird gave an ominous caw,
A death-like caw,) and I knew full well
That I was prey to some ancient spell.

3.

I crept to my bed
To bury my head
But the spirit invaded my brain
And my heart beat loud
As the spirit proud
Flooded my blood with pain,
Tortured my arteries, fluttered my sheet,
And prickled the veins in my weary feet,

I longed to swim through the lake of night
And lave in the water of living light.

4.

So at glint of day
I fled away
On the wings of the hurrying morn ;
As a murderer feels
His guilt at his heels
I knew that the spirit in scorn
Trod in my footsteps, laughed in my ears
And filled me with multitudinous fears.

5.

The silence around
Was too profound,
I hurried from flowers and trees,
The blackbird's note
Seemed too remote,
I was mad with the honey-fed bees ;
There was peace without, but a flame within
Kept leaping up from my heart of sin,
And the spirit fed the leaping fire
And fanned it higher, ever higher.

6.

So I sought the town
With its murky frown
And its mad humanity stored ;
And I reached a door,—
But the spirit swore
And the flames within me roared,
Roared like a furnace devouring the air
For I had my foot on the star-lit stair
That led me up to the Lord,
And I felt the spirit was pressing me down
From the sacred steps that led out of the town.

7.

Then a woman's eye
Like Love passed by,
And I heard her silk gown sing
With flitting grace
That left no trace,
Like a bird upon the wing,
And I hurried after the lovely sight,
I could not shake her free,
Like a curtain drawn across the night
She stood 'tween Heaven and me;
She stepped into my burning soul
And in the furnace seemed to roll,
And yet she burnt not but defied,
For sin her soul had deified

8.

Daintily fleet
Her pretty feet,
Her steps made not a sound,
As though a fay
Defied the day
And charmed the amorous ground,
She led me back to field and tree,
To all the wild bewitchery
Of rose and rainbow, rock and rill,
And music of the black-bird's bill,
She quenched my flames in floods of tears
And calmed my multitudinous fears.

9.

But alas, alas!
I felt her pass
Out of my soul like joy;
She came and went,
A sentiment
As transient as a toy,

And I was left
Of Love bereft
And I felt that the spirit in scorn
Laughed at my treachery, rifled my wit,
And as king and lord o'er my soul would sit.

10.

Then I took a pen
And wrote for men,
Told them the wail of my mind,
But they would not hear
The fall of my tear,
Deemed me both deaf and blind,
For what I had written the spirit had torn
Out of his mind from an age forlorn,
Far back in the Past in the realm of Death
And I but repeated his ancient breath.

11.

I looked with his eyes
And my lips' replies
In the gray of my brain he conceived,
I felt I was dead
In my own strange head,
I looked on the world and I grieved
That I could not deliver a thought of my own,
My laugh was another's, another's my groan.

12.

Then I said, "Away!
With this ancient play!"
And I bade the spirit,—"Adieu,
I have felt your fears
And shed your tears
But I now am myself and not you!"
And I saw him pass in the light of the moon
As an ancient mummy for ages aswoon!
I was free, I was free, I was flooded with joy
And I laughed into life with the heart of a boy.

TO MR T. H.

ON RECEIPT OF HIS COMPLIMENTARY LETTER OF
JUNE 5, 1899

PRAISE brings a sweet allurement; as a rose
   Held in a loving hand so comes to me
   Your note with fragrance of expectancy
And large, unwritten knowledge doth enclose.
Ne'er have I tried, in vanity, to pose
   As one who holds the mystic, tribal key
   To Man's high temples of philosophy;
But I have sought to please the soul that knows
The thrush's call, the dream of the blue-bell,
     The clouds that flirt with heaven, the Voice
      that springs
     Exultant from the eternal heart of things
To tell us wonders if we listen well.
May I have thousand friends like you to hear
If I be Nature's true interpreter

TO THE SAME

THY voice arises from the silent deep,
   Sounds through my being, wakes my poet-soul
   That, slowly smouldering, like a dying coal,
Now by thy breath of praise is blown from sleep:
Behold, the tiny flames begin to leap;
   Pile ore and fuel, mass the furnace high,
   Lift fire's red panoply into the sky,
Until the metal in a molten heap
Draws radiant wonder from the eyes around!
But dare I build on this enchanted ground
   My furnace of emotion, when I see
Into dull ash old temple-fires decay
   That once had coloured heaven, and on me
Once cast Fame's regal shadow of dismay?

THREE SONNETS ON THE FUTURE LIFE

SUGGESTED BY "X" IN "*THE ATHENÆUM*"
JAN. 4, 1902

Μέλλοντα ταῦτα

Not on sad Stygian shore, nor in clear sheen
Of far Elysian plain, shall we meet those
Among the dead whose pupils we have been,
Nor those great shades whom we have held as foes;
No meadow of asphodel our feet shall tread,
Nor shall we look each other in the face
To love or hate each other being dead,
Hoping some praise or fearing some disgrace:
We shall not argue, saying "'twas thus," or "thus":
Our argument's whole drift we shall forget;
Who's right, who's wrong, 'twill all be one to us,
We shall not even know that we have met.
    Yet meet we shall, and part, and meet again
    Where dead men meet, on lips of living men.

X.

I.

Your mind invades me as a frost; your scorn
    Clouds o'er my lilies' and my daisies' light,
    I feel your icy, pessimistic blight
Retard the advent of Man's promised morn:
But as Life's angel hovers in the corn,
    Wooes it with sun-lit Hope to fructify
    While carrier Death is slowly passing by,
So great imaginings in me are born:
And can I doubt these dreams and weakly sigh
    Myself into a mortal, while I feel
    Strange immortality upon me steal,
My spirit floating in some unknown sky?
Dare I to Nature say such hopes betray
Some magic liar haunting all my way?

2.

Not so, sad victim of material things :
    Your eyes have not the texture of the soul,
    Your ears hear not its music, as we roll
With the dear earth, fanned by ethereal wings
Into each day's new presence, which up-flings
    Its glory like a libertine abroad,
    And cuts out darkness with a magic sword.
List to the genius of the bird that sings ;
Hear him as he re-chants his way to heaven,
    Breaks through the brazen continent of clouds,
Soaring yet safe, by his great passion driven
    Above the thoughts that wrap themselves in
        shrouds ;
O! that this bird might in your being live
And give the spirit its prerogative !

3

Mayhap rich Nature in a variant mood
    Left you imperfect; wrapped you round and round
    With cloud, Hope may not enter, so profound
The dull material mist wherein you brood :
'Tis only thus you may be understood
    By one, like me, who dances in the blaze
    Of Hope's magnetic, Life-transfusing rays
That spanned the rainbow o'er old Noah's flood :
The very world to me is but a peak
    From which in keen expectancy I peer,
My inner ear can hear the Almighty speak,
    My inner eye beholds without a fear
Hope blow the earth's material cloud away
And bathe my spirit in a golden day !

AN EXHORTATION TO THE ANGLO-SAXON

O, ANGLO-SAXON men ! my dream of men !
Men of my heart !   O, let me beg in tears
That no dull idol may impede thy view
Of the great vital God within thy soul,
Who raised the violet for Man's eyes and made
For him Heaven's multitude of stars !
Brush Heaven away and trample on the rose,
Still the small chapel of thy soul will shrine
The *unseen* thought of Him.   We need no aid
To view the soul's eternities.   No priest,—
Much as I love each one,—can lead Man higher
By painted Virgin, shrines, or rosaries
That gently number lip-repeated prayers :
Only by clinging to the crags of Truth
Can a great priestly heart lift my small soul
Into the mountain-altitudes, where silent Thought
Sits brooding o'er the world, claiming divine
Dominion.   If, in aerial scales,
My thought-contented countrymen ! thy brain
May as a common ingot weigh a star,
Surely thy soul may by its reason rule
The sweet religion of mortality,
Seeing our souls are but magicians born
To populate the palaces to come !

THE HUMAN CRY

Zion cried, and Zion wept,
And, everyday, with Zion, I
Above the noisy village crept
And sang ourselves into the sky,
But not an answering Voice was sent
From that blue, cloud-weaving firmament ;
And yet there came a sigh, a breath,
A thought that never knew a death,
A touch that taught, a dream, a tear,
Out of that sacred atmosphere.

TO A MOTHER

In your white arms of Love you hold
  The offspring of a magic minute,
A babe more precious than fine gold
  Or song that flutters through a linnet.

O, lull it in your warm, white breast,
  Soothe it, fond mother, it is burning
For all the love but half expressed
  In this romantic vale of yearning!

It may be you are guarding there
  A saint who shall enchant the sinner,
A soul unconscious of despair,
  Of Hope's delusive heights the winner.

Whose ears with fine melodic sense
  May cull the music of our being,
Whose eyes with tenderness intense
  May claim the genius of seeing.

You know you hold in holy fear
  A little, soft recipient creature,
Whose lips will smile away a sneer
  And dimple Love in every feature.

Lull it, O mother, in your arms,
  Its joy prolongs our human story,
A little love of new-born charms,
  A sweet, inexplicable glory.

I kneel in wise idolatry
  To your aspiring baby mortal
And watch him with his hidden glee
  New bursting through Life's golden portal!

LIFE'S SULLIED HERITAGE

1.

'Tis not that I would climb or soar away,
  (There is a great rebellion in my soul,)
Far from the shadow of earth's clouded Day,
  To where sweet Light unfolds its golden scroll ;

2

But that some flattering charm might change distress
  In Time's wild garden ; so that I may be
Not as mute stone in Man's wide wilderness,
  But, like a rose-bud, fragrant, pure and free,

3.

Feeding itself on sunlight and blue sky,
  In loving sympathy with bowers of green,
And crimson of the morn, and clouds that fly
  In breezy indolence o'er heaven's blue screen.

4.

No rose could flourish in an air defiled,
  'Twould gaze reproachfully on each new Spring ;
Nor can I joy until sweet Life has smiled,
  And Love has taught each aching heart to sing.

5.

I look around, and lo ! Man's cruel hand
  Binds round his brother's wrist a bond of steel,
Still do the rich in ignorance expand,
  Still hunger treadeth at the poor man's heel,

6.

And still our children's children feel the touch,
  The sullying touch of those who went before,
Who nursed their souls in sensual arms too much
  And struck in drunken frolic at Death's door,

7.

And smote fair Beauty, so that she lay dead,
  And never eye could find her in the fields,
Or see her blush upon her rainbow-bed,
  For only to the sun of Love she yields.

8.

Men pass me by with faces worn and weak,
  As tho' by some mad Inquisition scared,
Vainly for sweet fresh Beauty may I seek,—
  And yet, I know, God has in Man appeared.

9.

A conscious knowledge veils the maiden's eye,
  A too material bible dulls our youth;
We thrill too much with senses born to die
  For Beauty in our life to flower to Truth.

10.

Yet, Nature, thou art ever firm and true,
  For, if our careless footstep crush thy flower,
Thou wilt the lovely angel-form renew,
  A perfect wonder in a happier hour!

11

Oh ! for thy spirit-wind to cleanse mankind
  As thou dost scatter far the foetid air,
Thy Wintry frost to nip the prurient mind,
  Thy Spring to flower anew thoughts fresh and fair !

12.

For then the day would dawn, I know full well,
  When Man with Beauty would his birthright grace,
And priests of Purity with potent spell
  Would purge brutality from thought and face.

13.

When, now, we look for Beauty, o'er our eyes
  A misty picture falls that hides the real,
Like blackened boughs that fright the summer skies
  The healthful sap of Life we do not feel.

14.

Or why should we be wanton with our tears,
  Or fill frail trumpets with our murderous breath,
Or bury nations in a tomb of fears,
  Or tremble at the pageant of grim Death?

15.

I picture forth the healthful spring of Life
  That issued, pure, from Eden's fairy dream,
Where Eve stood wondering o'er its bubbling strife,
  And saw her face reflected in the stream;

16.

And sad am I to know that 'mid cool green,
  It might have down the years unsullied rolled,
If Man to his great trust had faithful been,
  And had not to black Vice its water sold.

17.

Then should our eyes in full entrancement see
  Man's beauteous face lit with enraptured mind;
Ne'er should we hear him sigh and own, though free,
  He leaves a record riotous behind.

18.

I see new poets look in Heaven's blue eye
   And slander God with busy gallfull tongue;
For ever asking the Almighty why
   They were by serpent Evil coiled and stung?

19.

Forgetful that God made them free as air
   To woo the holy or to wallow deep
In miry, lustful dungeons of Despair,
   Where like low toads, upon their breast they creep.

20.

Why fight we still, and cheat, and lie, and curse,
   And in pursuit of Evil wax so brave?
Why do new Cains walk, callous, by the hearse
   That bears their murdered brother to the grave?

21.

Why do the nations shake the world with fear
   When human passion rises, like the sea,
Boiling and surging, 'till wild waves appear
   That break against the rock of Destiny?

22.

Why? Why? my brothers, when we know full well
   That Love is like an ever watchful bride
Who waits to lure us from the subtle spell
   Of tempter Evil crawling by our side.

23

Love! that, when fondled, like a babe will spring
   To hopeful manhood from his mother's arms,
And, in profusion, will rich blessings fling
   To those who fondly nurse his tender charms.

24.

Love ! that the Cross charmed to a living tree
Which waves its blossoms o'er the gathering years,
Where each poor soul, who mounts his Calvary,
May gather fruit and lose delirious fears

25.

Love ! that made wise men glean the fields of Time
Heaping their treasures for the heirs unborn,
Gaining with reverent eyes a glimpse sublime
Of Man's mysterious, ever-coming Morn ;

26.

So that no pilgrim through this world may plead
That he bewildered was, when, on his way,
He chose from Nature's hand the poisoned weed,
And scorned her wholesome flowers' fair display ;

27.

Or deem that he may toss his magic mind
As worthless matter in his delved grave,
Or label o'er his soul that he is blind
And float, a hypocrite, o'er Death's wild wave !

28.

Why should we leave, in shame, our mother Earth
Polluted by our sordid, sensual dreams ?
Fair flowers should mark the advent of our birth,
Fed and illumined by our spirit-gleams !

29.

And yet we idly view our brother's woe,
And pass him by in stiff, affected pride,
As though there were divisions here below,
And cynic Heav'n had taught us Love, and—lied !

M

30.

Oh! brothers! brothers! if th' Almighty hand,
    That made us Man, descended in rebuke
To crush the Earth, 'til not a grain of sand
    Might mark the reckless human course it took,

31.

Could Justice lift her finger and complain,
    Or bid God spare us from the righteous blow;
Like puling poets, callous or insane,
    Singing Agnostic verses here below?

32.

No! No! with one great voice, we fain must own
    That we have been unworthy and have spoiled
The heritage of Joy we might have known
    Had we not lain with tempter Evil coiled.

33.

Behold! in apathy the poppied East
    Still dreams the Future veils a bed of sleep,
While the new, sleepless West, with Light increased
    Only pretends a love for Christ to keep!

34.

And all the storied archives of the Wise
    Have builded been for our strange world in vain,
New, shallow minds the ancient wit despise,
    And fill the listening Universe with pain!

35.

Come then, ripe Time, and cleanse our sensual sin,
    Till toiling flesh be pure as Nature's flowers,
That we may for new generations win
    Emancipation from polluted hours.

36.

I see, in dream, the idols of the Past
    Crumble to naught in thy destroying hands,
And walls uprise of Love's cathedral vast
    To which pure priests come flocking from all lands,

37.

While clouds of guilt are from the Present blown
    Into the Past by Love's creative breath,
'Till not a tender sorrow here is known
    Or the delusive agony of death.

38.

But men walk, pure as angels, glad with song,
    And women, beauteous as are flowers in June,
Cling close beside them, in gay festal throng,
    Singing in triumph earth's new bridal tune!

39.

And then, in those fair days, these heartfelt cries,
    Rent from my bosom by my brothers' tears,
Will be dull ancient sermons to new eyes
    Who come to read me in the gathering years.

THE GARDEN OF WHITE FLOWERS

REPENTANCE

1.

To this fair garden, once, in tears I came;
    Here I, again, in penitence return,
Remorseful-sad to think the world should claim
    This heart that still for tenderness doth yearn.

2.

It is a spot enclosed with high, mossed wall,
   O'er which no prying, vandal eyes may peer,
And in its verdurous heart a waterfall
   Makes murmurous music to the thrush's ear,

3.

And wanders idly to the river deep
   That laps with languorous lips the shelving ground :
So still the hush, a soul might wake from sleep
   Fearing the fan of bee a trumpet sound.

4.

A holy place it is of sunlit air,
   In which an abbey nestles, lost in dream
Of time-old memories, monk, and Virgin-fair,
   And God in mist of superstitious gleam.

5.

A box-tree, like a black Diocesan,
   And solemn yew-trees, grouped, like funeral mutes,
Mourn silently ; although no coffined-man
   Has ever yet enriched their gloomy roots.

6.

They mourn, alas ! the unrepentant Mind,
   (Whom cruel Evil draws for ever down,)
Which has no rest, but like a startled hind
   Seems ever followed by a fancied frown.

7.

Here flees the warrior-heart to mourn for sin,
   (That rages round him like a martyr's flame,)
Luring to light the tears that well within,
   And pain his bosom with a noble shame.

8.

And as he kneels upon the sacred ground,
  To add his tribute-tears to God's great sea
Of unrequited Sorrow; lo! around
  The fruitful tears white flowers arise in glee.

9.

These he may gather in a posie pure,
  And wear in his true bosom while the day
Of delicate Repentance may endure;
  That gone; they vanish like a tear away.

10.

Sweet the delight of priest or maiden-fair
  When from this garden of white flowers they speed,
Clad in the saintly floral-gown of Prayer,
  While on the heart of Love they inly feed.

11.

But sad the eyes that see the fresh flowers fade
  When in their bosom creeps the rifling thought,
That robs them of the peace the flowers had made,
  The tender ecstasy their tears had bought.

12.

(A wild, weird wilderness our heart may be,
  Or a sweet, flowering garden of delight!
A shadow-haunted mist of misery,
  Or a great sun to chase away the night!)

13.

But in this garden, now, I bend my knees
  And with my gracious tears white-flowers beget,
That shall no more be my pale perjuries,
  And with their withered leaves my conscience fret.

14.

And from this quiet spot, I, happy, go,
  Thro' groves of walnut-trees, whose limbs I see
Writhing in air, as though some fiend below
  Twisted their limbs with pain perpetually.

15.

'Neath their tormented arms I walk in peace,
  Wearing in pride my emblem of white flowers,
Sure that my Tempter's triumphs now shall cease
  And I may measure his diminished powers!

TELL ME, LITTLE SPARROW!

1.

TELL me, little sparrow,
  With the ne'er shut eye,
If Heaven's gate be narrow
  In the wall of sky?

2.

With thy wings' wild glory
  Search afar and near,
Tell me if the hoary
  With the young appear?

3.

If Mahomet's heroes
  With the Hindoo saints,
Press by waiting Neroes
  While the Christian faints?

4.

Tell me all the wonder
  That man's brain propounds,
Tell me of the Thunder
  And the earthquake-sounds:

5.

Go! and still the doubtings
Of my little mind,
Plagued by angry shoutings
Of the dull and blind!

6.

But the sparrow chirrupped :—
"Naught doth puzzle me,
When the apple's syrupped
Falls it from the tree,

7.

"When the blossomed roses
Die upon the stem
In the seed reposes
Yet a lovelier gem.

8.

"I see nothing narrow
In the deep blue sky
But my brother sparrow
Who thinks all must die,

9.

"Like the selfish mortal
Who would shut a friend
From the Heaven's wide portal
When this life doth end;

10.

"As though he were better
For his narrow creed
Than the love-begetter
In the hour of need.

11.

"What the gleaner leaveth
　On the fields of gold
My frail life receiveth,
　And the canon bold

12.

"I have seen in pity
　Written on the earth
Endeth this quaint ditty :—
　Death is but a Birth."

MY DISCARDED BODY

THROW the dread thing away!　So strange it is,
So pitiless, so cold; and with glazed eyes
Torments my soul with its effrontery!
It is not I; it is a mask I wore,
A marionette that on the stage of life
Danced as my fancy bade.　It laughed and cried
And copied me so well that it is now
Mistaken for myself; but to conceive
That mummy my sane self is to my mind
An evidence, indeed, of mind deranged.
But am I sure?　Did that form play with me
Or I with it?　Was he the master; I
The hired man?　When I with his false lips dared kiss
That trustful maiden, was it he or I
That smote the heart of the observing God,
Who values Love as once I valued gold?
Was it he or I who robbed my brother,
Cursed and smote at Justice, tore down laws
And cast them to Oblivion, and still dared
To walk, with upright mien, before my friends?
Was it he or I who wondered at the stars,
And said with wisdom-air there is no God,

Saw only the material life of man,
And ate and drank till cheeks grew rubicund,
And wit fell low as the most serious ape's
Humouring a gazing crowd?   Was it he or I
Who said he could not hear the awful Voice
Speak in the solemn chamber of my soul,
Who laughed soft tears away, and laid his limbs
Limp on the couch of selfishness?   Was it he
Or I that drowned my delicacy deep,
That soiled th' unsullied bloom upon my soul,
That lured my brother to the evil thing,
And, fearless, laughed at the audacity?
Alas ! alas !   I fear that it was I ;
I was the master, he the hired man !

Yet it was he that said :—"To be or not
To be? that is the question : " (for I AM
And must for ever BE :) but he was oft
Tired of the mummery of Life and would
Have lain him down upon the road, as he
Lies now, but for my will.   Poor Marionette !

He had strange ways with him.   At times when I
Was seated on a mountain hearing God
Discourse with mighty voice to listening stars
Amid the summer lightning, he would rise
And play wild freaks before my awe-struck soul.
He would paint pictures to my maddened gaze
Of lovely women luring me to earth
With eyes beneath long lashes languishing !
Or he would build me castles filled with wealth,
But garrisoned by Evil's wily knaves
Calling aloud to me their ranks to join,
Where splendour, luxury, and selfish joys
Were for the mercenary soldier spread !
Yes : 'twas at such high moments he would come
And freakishly torment me with his lusts.

My Discarded Body

His lusts ! indeed, *not mine*, whose soul can soar
Through all the universe, as doth a bee
From flower to flower upon the honied earth,
Whose thought the globe can pierce and see the sun
Shine on the fair Antipodes ; whose mind
Can conjure up immeasurable dreams
And holy aspirations, far beyond
The dull-eyed entertainment of this Mask.

We were great friends : and I was grieved when pain
Swept down on him from some great wind of God
To torture him, and make him limp in tears
For his wild sins !   And once he drank a cup
Drawn from the brook that prattled purity
Which he had soiled, and lo ! the fever came,
Like a hot whirlwind from the furnace mouth
Of the red sun, and wild delirium tore
The marionette's weak brain.   The fever past,
How sweet it was with convalescent steps
To walk with him, and hear his ample voice
Tell me how vain his animal delights
Had been to him ; how wiser I, who looked
For something more than the decaying earth,
And saw God's presence in me ; needing not
The Bible, or the talk of man, to aid my soul,
Which is a revelation to itself
Yet, when restored, he once again contrived
To lure me into new entanglements
That tore my soul and made my steps afraid
To walk in the Great Presence that I saw.

Sad-eyed, he said : " Tush ; you are born to die ;
There is a venom in the world that kills,
And there's no healer with an anodyne ; "
But 'twas all scorn, his new-born sentient scorn ;
The Mighty Presence was a magic world
Beyond his comprehension or his dream.

The tragedy is o'er; put the Mask by:
'Tis a dread thing whose clammy touch I fear.
But yet the play had taught my novice steps
To walk with confidence a nobler part,
In lovelier scenes; where Life's great dream grows
  clear
And clouds of Doubt for ever disappear.

INVOCATION TO SPRING

1.

Oh! tender, flower-clad Spring,
Once more I hear thee sing
Thy glad, sweet, new-born melodies of praise;
What a light heart I feel
As to thy dress I kneel,
What sunlit Hope laughs thro' thy blue-eyed gaze!

2.

What fairy-haunted bowers,
What frolic of sweet flowers,
What magic fingers and what busy brain!
What deep, religious notes
Mellow thy black-birds' throats,
What green-gold meadows full of sun and rain!

3.

Thy mind the branches taught
Their new green leaves of Thought,
As each fresh bud lost fear of daunting snows
And burst from Winter's hand
To smile upon the land,
Wooed by thy loveliness from dead repose.

4.

I thank thee for thy may,
For thy blown apple spray,
For fleeting lilac and for cowslip-gold,
For tulip and blue-bell,
For violets in the dell,
For roses that thy dying hands unfold

5.

Thy dying hands! Ah! yes!
Even thy smiles that bless
Must fade away as doth a sunset hue,
We cannot keep thee here
To still our Wintry fear
When frozen tears storm down the clouded blue.

6.

Would I, like thee, O Spring,
Could ope my lips and sing,
Could close my eyes and feel the joy again
Of those great dreams of yore,
In that divine Before,
Ere sword of sorrow clove my heart in twain.

7.

Ere the peach-bloom was lost,
Ere Conscience felt Death's frost,
Ere the Spring-thought was seared with Autumn
    brown,
Ere the rill fell to earth
Forgetting its pure birth,
And, sullied, rolled in lazy languor down.

8.

I would be held by thee
In flowered captivity,

And, like a rainbow, blossom in thy skies,
Like thee I would be young,
Rose-thoughts upon my tongue,
And light of lilies shining from mine eyes !

9.

The name that I have signed
Can never be divined
As mine upon the tablets of the earth,
It is some other name
Forged in an hour of shame,
Not that made sacred at my solemn birth.

10.

Lend me Redemption's pen
To blot that name from men,
And write my true one in rich, liquid gold ;
A name that I may show,
As 'twere a flower below,
With honied virtue hidden in each fold.

12.

But Oh ! sweet Spring, I hear
From him who keeps a sneer
To cut to tears the tender heart of things,
That thou hast never seen
A Spirit in the green
Who made thee and thy thousand sister Springs ;

12.

That the veined leaf was planned
By the alchemic sand
Inspired to action by the thinking sea,
That lilies rose full-blown
Untutored from the stone,
Whence Man came forth to dream of the To Be.

13.

Toss all thy flowers away,
Fair Spring ! and be not gay
If such be the sad burden of thy leaves ;
Let a stiletto dart
Out of the sky's great heart
To silence him who this dull thought conceives !

14.

No wintry tongue shall e'er
Thy soaring thoughts ensnare,
Thou gentle garlander of waking boughs ;
Thou seest the unseen
Conceiver in the green,
Who with fair promise every branch endows !

15.

Therefore to me, O Spring,
Thou art a sacred thing,
The prophet-preacher of the passing year
What sunburnt Summer gives
She but from thee receives,
And Autumn is but thine executor ;

16.

E'en Winter but apes Death,
With resurrection breath,
Time-old preserver of Life's thousand forms,
Who loves to see thee grace
With flowers his surly face,
Thou bold defier of the breath of storms !

17.

As each new year comes round
Thou springest from the ground

With floral passion never born to die;
    And in thy flowers concealed
    We find the Autumn yield,
And watch thee sweep Despair from Heaven's blue
    sky.

18.

    Yet one said to my heart
    That Life and I must part;
And much I wondered that men deemed him wise
    And gilded large his name
    Within their house of Fame,—
That haunt of bat-blind thoughts and buried lies.

19.

    For I, O Spring, like thee
    Have Immortality,
As flowers live on for aye from seed to seed;
    But there's a lovelier thing
    Locked in this flesh, O Spring,
Than ever eyes have seen in thy gay mead:

20.

    A great, ethereal sprite
    That peers into the Night
And waiteth for the coming of the Dawn,
    Pluming his wings to soar
    When Death unbars the door
And bids him flee where all the rest have gone:

21.

    A soul that may expand
    Or wither in Life's hand,
Longing for higher Life or Death's decay;
    A theatre so vast
    Where all the boundless Past
And all the Future have wide space for play;

22.

And yet a sacred shrine
Where lips with words divine
Soft litanies of dreaming love intone ;
Where angel Truth defies
The eloquence of Lies,
Both pleading in my heart in Silence lone :

23

A passion, like the sea
Lifted tumultuously
With snow-white billows 'gainst th' unfeeling shore ;
And a deep calm, like Death,
Without creative breath,
Lost in the dismal hollow of earth's core

24.

A pain that pierceth deep
Through the soft bed of sleep
Like lightning quivering from a summer cloud ;
And a great pleasure born
Light as the rosy morn
Leaps in fresh beauty from Night's dismal shroud.

25.

O Spring ! all things am I,
A joy, a hope, a sigh ;
A phantom seeking an imagined light ;
A conqueror, a slave ,
A delver of a grave,
A wing-heeled climber of the mountain-height ;

26.

A trouble, and a peace ;
A craver for release,

Yet tender loath to bid the world farewell;
Born both to scorn and praise;
To sleep and yet to gaze;
To image forth a heaven and forge a hell;

27.

A sinner and a saint;
Strong, yet most weak and faint;
My own strange opposite, as though I were
In mystery involved;—
A being unresolved
Whether to die in flesh or float in air.

28.

Can such a wonder own
A father in a stone,
And have no hope but with this earth to roll
Law-bound to the great sun,
Now as a wondering one,
Then as a corpse beneath her grassy knoll?

29.

I, who, in stillness, feel
Wild music thro' me steal
When soft, mysterious, unseen fingers play
Upon my passion-strings
Wild, sweet, immortal things,
Too sacred for a mortal lip to say!

30.

No! I will virtue sip
From Nature's honied lip
And kiss thee, maiden Spring, until I share
Thine innocence and glee,
And, when divinely free,
I'll leave my form to mother Earth's kind care,

N

31.

And wander far away
Into a lovelier Day,
Where my new life shall have an astral Spring;
Where temples of the Mind,
By fairy Thought designed,
Dwarf with their splendour each material thing!

32.

As a loved babe in arms
Lives on its mother's charms
So thou the virtue sippeth from Earth's breast;
While I, a baby sprite,
In Spirit take delight,
And know that I am far more nobly blest.

33.

Ah me! it were as vain
To stay the sun-made rain
As to deny the human mind its dream;
Vain to think dungeon-Death
Can stifle spirit-breath,
Or that the pall of Night can hide Heaven's gleam:

34.

For from Night's diamonds shine
Bright thoughts of the divine
That are not false to Nature or to me;
Hope dreams that colour joy,
Not like a transient toy
Used but to make the dreary moments flee!

35.

Hark! I can hear Death's bell
Sound forth my funeral knell,

While thou, once more, art robed in all thy flowers,
    And to the human throng
    Again doth sing thy Song
That I have heard thro' all my mortal hours ;

36.

    The Song that comes from far,
    Beyond the furthest star,
Wrung from the heart of the Creator-Mind ;—
    The Mind that bids thee rise
    An ever-new surprise
To priest, creed-clouded, or to layman, blind.

37.

    To that great·Song I march
    Beneath Life's bright blue arch,
Past my dull funeral rites, until the gleam
    Of wide, celestial light
    Bursts on my new-born sight,
More wondrous than unfathomable dream.

TO THE UNKNOWN PROPRIETOR OF A WOOD MARKED "PRIVATE, TRESPASSERS WILL BE PROSE-CUTED"

WOULD you shut your wood from me
Where my thrushes claim their tree,
Where my tender black-bird's call
Holds the earth and heaven in thrall?
Why should you so vandal be,
You, who boast yourself as free?

O! they call me; I must go!
For my soul doth love them so,

196   To the Proprietor of a Wood

And I pass your threatening board
By "Authority" adored :
(I do not adore, I fret
That my freedom you forget,)
For I would no flower despoil
Peeping through *my* amorous soil.

The rabbits, when your footfall comes,
Hurry from you as from drums
When fantastic fingers beat
Warlike music for the feet,
But they come to me like fawns
Stepping o'er the silent lawns
When to them I kindly bring
Delicate Love's offering,
Love's indenture calls them mine
Though the parchments bear your sign.

If your feelings were as fine
As your rabbits', who now mine
Tunnel-room without a fee,
Without a miner's royalty,
Would you not forbear to fence
My wood with your vain opulence?

If you came each day to peep
At *my* flowers, I should weep
As I do when I behold
A morbid soul gloat o'er his gold,
Though I should not feel surprise
That you shut them from my eyes,
But as you go never there
To see my frozen rose despair,
'Tis like hiding God's own stars
With a gold roof bound with bars.

LATE SPRING

FAIR Spring is late;
Her tired feet wait
At the sun's gold-temple gate;
Lingering for the soft, warm air,
Ere venturing into dresses fair.
Dresses of blossoms that must fade
Fast as the subtle twilight shade
Falls on the cloud-blooms of the sun,
Heedless of all the wonders done!
The trees are bare
But for bold budding here and there;
Shy peeping tints of green,
And gummy globes of red
Cradling the chesnut blossoms in warm bed,
While through the branches blow
Cold gusts of wind and shivering flakes of snow.
Upon the elms a strange, dull red
Creeps o'er the branches ere they spread
Their life into a robe of green
With sunlight glancing in between.
The blue-bell hath not followed yet
The sweet alluring violet,
But beneath the cheerless trees
See! the bright anemones
Weave o'er all last year's brown leaves
Delicate embroideries!

NATURE ONE WITH MY SOUL IN SPRINGTIME

THE damson-trees, the cherries, and the pears
  Have risen like white-angels from the gloom;
    And what a joy is theirs
  Silently dreaming in their robes of bloom!

198 Song of a Heart of the City

The sparrow celebrates their white display
    In chirrups blown abroad ;
But the great thrush sings a diviner lay,
    (He is the mighty minstrel of the Lord,)
And o'er their floral tributes of delight
Doth careless carols cunningly indite,
    Each note more lovely than my chosen word.
    The raptures of the trees and of the bird
    Have the deep being of my nature stirred ;
    The blossoms from my bosom seem to blow,
    My voice is in the songster of the branches,
    Upon the sea of clouds that come and go
    My floatful spirit gloriously launches,
        The magic sun
    Sinks with my soul into a floral fire,
        The day is done
And in my sleep the world and I expire,
        Only to rise
Each day into a lovelier surprise

SONG OF A HEART OF THE CITY

ON HOLIDAY IN THE COUNTRY

I AM a heart of the City, seeking the green,
Seeking the soul of the mountain, and the loved sheen
Flossed on the breast of the ocean from the soft eyes
Peeping behind the eternal veil of the skies.
Here throbs my heart in its pleasure all the long day,
Seeming to soar far above me, ever away
Far from the thrall of the body, in a great dream,
'Till from the soul of the Universe bursts a bright gleam
Touched by the frost of the moonlight, telling my sight
What the deep thinking of Nature tells to the Night.
Have I not felt with the sunbeam ?   Have I not joyed
In the red roses' pure blushes ?   Love unalloyed !

Has not the voice of the linnet told to my ear
Secrets eternally welcome, tenderly dear?
Have I not rushed with the whirlwind up the steep
    side
Of the dark crag as it frowneth o'er valleys wide,
And watched it hold sport with the eagle, higher and
    higher
'Till a black cloud in the firmament flashed forth its
    fire,
Thundered and burst in a torrent over the plain,
Cheering the sun-stricken meadow with the cool rain?
Have I not seen on that mountain many a stream
Laugh in its babyhood, babble, and fall, like cream,
Into a lap of heather, ruddy as sanguine Morn
When it breaks from its night-dark curtains, to ripen
    the whispering corn?
Has not the soft-spoken snow-drop sung to the sun
Out of the cold heart of Winter? Has it not won
Pæans of praise from the poets as in its face
They have beheld the eternal spirit of grace,—
Spirit of innocent beauty, like a pure bride,
Wed to the passionate violet thrown by its side?
Oh! I have joyed in the Silence while the red orb
Laid in a rose-bed of splendour seemed to absorb
All the great thought of Creation, all that uprose
As the Sun-Father of Nature sank to repose.
And in that Silence I've wandered far into space,
Over the mountains of trouble, 'till not a trace
Of sorrow, and anguish, and crying came to my
    ears,
And I, a mortal triumphant, cleft from my fears,
Sang a grand hymn in the Silence up to the throne
Of Him who Presideth above me; then have I known
Exaltings, and far-away-whispers, silent decrees,
Sounding eternally present, as on my knees
I bowed to the Spirit-Pervading. Then have I gone
Back to the heart of the City, as a young fawn

Glides to his flock in the valley, better I ween
For the ecstatic communings with the cool green,
And with that magical mountain, where I have soared
While the great tide of Humanity 'neath me has
    roared

SONG OF A HEART OF THE COUNTRY

ON HOLIDAY IN THE CITY

I AM a heart of the country, seeking the town,
Seeking the soul of Humanity, 'neath the dark frown
Of the smoke of the nostrils of Labour, as he lifts high
Shoulders of magical energy into the sky.
The sun, that flirts with the flowers and varies the
    green,
Swims by in the blue lake above us unheeded, unseen,
And eyes that were born for the beautiful see not at
    all
The moon's gay ribbons of silver flutter and fall ;
The clouds that float like the fleece of the lambs of
    heaven,
And the stars in the empire of Night from the zenith
    are driven,
Yet the eye of the town beholds not the ways of the
    skies
But lives in its vision tumultuous of laughter and sighs,
Shutting the sun-fire from heaven, mocking the moon,
With millions of luminous lanterns outvying noon.
Here as I float with my brothers thro' Thought's deep
    sea
Feel I a wave from the Ages break over me,
Scattering its passion and impulse, flowering in foam,
As an Atlantic's great billow bursts 'neath Heaven's
    dome
All the great Past seems behind me, pressing me on,
Ages all hoary with Wisdom, spectral and wan,

And ages that pelt me with flowers, plucked from the
fields
Of Springtime, impatient with Summer and slow
Autumn yields.
Lone in the country I feel not the struggle of Life,
Miss the great sea of existence fretted with strife,
But here I thrill with emotion all the long day
Watching the great hull of Destiny crush its stern way
Through floating shoals of Humanity clutching the
waves,
Kingless, ungoverned, unbridled, weak, aimless slaves.
Yet know I well a Controller rules over all,
Lord of the tempest and torrent, holding in thrall
The great, poised earth with its wonders, so that no day,
Tho' it have naught to commend it, passeth away
Unheeded, forgotten, or scorned; yea, as I see
Hurrying brothers pass by me, flippantly free,
Who with the hands of the wanton break the fair shrine
In the true heart of a maiden,—flower-like, divine,—
Seem I to see th' Almighty flash from the skies
Lightning of terrible anger from His dark eyes.
I would my mountain of silence bring from afar,
Or from the garden of heaven pluck a fair star
To awe the crowd with mute wonder that they might
feel
How to the works of Creation mortals must kneel!
Yea; I would ask them my questions;—" Whither
away?
Ye who know naught of the lilies' tender display?
Heedless of stars in the firmament and the gold sun,
Ye who in mazes of Mammon helplessly run?
Whither away, ye gay-dressed ones? Is there no deep
Where the great soul of Humanity falleth asleep?
Must ye be restless for ever, troubled with care,
And of the peace of fair Nature live unaware?"
Thy answer defiant salutes me, as on ye flee :—
" God has no vision of glory opened to me,

To-day but foretells to-morrow, all are the same,
Life doth but light up, and flicker, and die like a
 flame ! "
Ah ! let the breath of Creation winnow thy tongue,
And thy philosophy hard from thy reason be flung ,
Love in rebellious emotion stifles thy scream,
Bids thee in sweetness remember Life's precious
 dream,
Hope's happy glimpse from the mountains, and the
 wide range
O'er which the mind of man travels trembling and
 strange ;
All the stirred depths of thy feelings loud to thee call,
God has a vision of glory opened to all !
Ah ! thou art deaf to my language ! Why am I vain,
Thrusting my duller intelligence on thy bright brain?
I, who have lumbered thro' knowledge ! I, who delight
To hear thy gay laugh, Oh, Humanity, waken the
 Night,
And go to thy play-house to watch thee hold up to
 scorn
Treachery, meanness, and fear,—of vulgarity born !
Greater art thou than my mountain ; yet thy vain crowd
Reckless, impatient of knowledge, confident, loud,
Need a great standard to lead them, having no sun
To light them each day to the halls of the Governing
 One.
While I pass back to the love that I see in the flowers,
Map thou thy pathway to heaven thro' thy turbulent
 hours ,
I will unfold to the stars the fine fabric of thought
Spun from thy multitude-mind, with fair jewels in-
 wrought ;
And I may conjure, mayhap, a new dream in the skies,
Which, but for sojourn with thee, had been blank to
 my eyes.

MUSIC AT DEATH

1.

I CAN hear a minstrel wailing,
  Gently wailing by the sea,
Solemn-sweet his deep emotion,
  Music beautiful to me.

2.

Dimly in the mask of twilight,
  Just beneath yon glowing star,
I can see the minstrel gazing,
  While his music floats afar.

3.

Hark! the music nearer cometh,
  He approacheth like a dream,
With a trooping band of angels
  Clad in white, and gold, and cream.

4.

And the music slowly changeth,
  Wailing sounds no more I hear,
But a melody of triumph
  Falls on my enchanted ear;

5.

Throbbing to the marching angels
  As they in procession glide,
Till they stay their mystic progress
  And are chanting close outside.

6.

Oh! what melodies appealing
  They are singing at the door,
Throw it open wide and bid them
  Sing them sweetly o'er and o'er.

7.

Hear you not the mystic music?
See you not the minstrel-band?
As you by my side are sadly
Clinging to my dying hand.

8.

See you not the angels bending
'Neath the weight of my white bark,
Into which my soul doth enter
As I glide into the Dark?

9.

You will take this form when lifeless
And in pomp of funeral grieve,
And will bid some minstrel artist
Tender lamentations weave,

10.

But, remember, I am sailing
O'er the deep mysterious sea,
With the angels round me chanting
Music beautiful to me.

BABY ENCHANTING

BABY enchanting, lulled in my breast,
Locked in the calm of thy haven of rest,
Moans on the ocean of Life I can hear,
Mournful sweet moaning too sad for thine ear,
Baby enchantingly dear !

In bells of the lily thy honey is stored,
The broad blade of grass is thy fanciful sword,
The spill of gold-straw is thy shivering spear,
And coral leaps up from the deep for thee, dear,
Silently sleep, I am near.

The gold-belted buttercup serves as thy ship,
The wand of the willow thy whimsical whip,
Old Time's ticking watch comes to tickle thine ear,
To lure thee to laughter, my own baby dear,
Smile in thy sleep, I am near.

Play with old Time in thine innocent way,
Till to thy soul the high mountains shall say ;—
" Gaze from our heights till thy Vision appear ! "
Glory shall bloom for thee, then, baby dear,
Glory I may not be near.

But thy mind I'll festoon with Love's holiest flowers
To bear thee ripe fruit in Life's trouble-tossed hours,
When eyes of Temptation shall fill thee with fear,
And I am not nigh thee to aid thee, my dear,
Sleep, darling, while I am near.

SYMPATHY

GRIEVED have I seen a flower
Broken at the stem
Dying hour by hour,
Lovely, bruised gem !
But I've passed my brother
Crushed like this fair bloom,
Passed him with another
Heedless of his doom ;
Never saw his glances
Looking into mine,
Like reproachful lances
Cutting mine and thine ,
Never gave him heeding,
Never wondered why
His poor heart was bleeding
While I knew no sigh.

THE YEARNING FOR PERFECTION

1.

Can you tell me why I'm yearning
  Ever yearning for a Light
Far above me, far beyond me,
  Steadfast, pure, and bright ?

2.

If I see a face of Beauty,—
  Beauty dimpled with a smile,—
Still a lovelier, holier phantom
  Will my soul beguile.

3

If I view the gold-sun dying
  On a purple, crimson bed,
Lovelier pictures flit before me
  By sweet Fancy fed.

4.

If I o'er a chasm standing
  Gaze into the dark abyss,
I can see more awful visions,
  More sublime than this

5.

I can stand 'tween Earth and Heaven,
  Marshal angels to my side,
Armed with lightning, voiced with thunder,
  With high Thought I ride.

6.

As I walk the boundless region
  Open to immortal Mind,
Nothing seems to daunt the daring
  Of the soul refined.

7.

So I dream that I am destined,
  When I fall upon my bier,
To be led, as Fancy leads me,
  Far away from here.

8.

Where the yearnings of my spirit,
  Shall their true ideals see,
Lovelier than my sweet earth-mother
  Can reveal to me.

A WORD

A SOFT sweet word of Life's morning,
  Told with a tear,
Breaking a phalanx of scorning,
  Entered my ear;

Entered, and set my soul dreaming,
  Lifted me high,
Out of my sordid-earth-scheming,
  Into the sky!

Yet a wild word on the morrow,
  Told by a jade
Stirring a cauldron of sorrow,
  Made me afraid.

Bore down the lovely emotion,
  Held me to earth,
And in Life's treacherous ocean
  Drowned my new birth.

Come down thou soul of the Silence,
  Dumb thou our tongue,
'Till from its red Throne of Violence
  Evil be flung!

THE WEDDING OF GOODNESS AND HAPPINESS

1.

WHEN will thy marriage be? sweet friends of mine;
   I hear Love's wedding-chimes blown down the vale
   'Mid nuptial-songs of thrush and nightingale
But never thine, sweet friends, but never thine!

2.

Thy troth was plighted with Love's tongue divine,
   So I have heard from all the treasured dead,
   And I of fair espousals oft have read,
But ne'er of thine, sweet friends, but ne'er of thine!

3.

I asked a priest if e'er the sun would shine
   Upon thy wedding-day?   He gazed afar
   And dreamed he viewed the marriage of a star,
But never thine sweet friends, but never thine!

4.

He said thy bridal-bond no priest could sign,
   The record would be stainèd with his name,
   His hand would tremble, he would blush for shame;
So never thine, sweet friends, so never thine!

5.

But happier I; for down Hope's radiant line
   I see in splendour pass a wedding fair
   'Mid song and dance and happy sunlit air,
And it is thine, sweet friends, and it is thine!

6.

Crown with finality this vision fine,
   So that earth's wedding-bells may clang in glee,
   And every marriage of two hearts may be
Thine, my sweet friends, ever and ever thine!

TO THE MEMORY OF

CHARLES EDWARD TROUGHTON,

Chief Cashier of Lloyd's Bank, Margate ;
and Superintendent of Margate Ambulance Corps,
who always went in the rescuing
boat to lend his aid to shipwrecked sufferers.
Lost in the capsizing of the serf-boat
" Friend of all Nations "
in a great storm at Margate, December 2nd, 1897.

HONOUR, honour to him be
Who has thrown into the sea
Life for Immortality !
  Life ! for brother man !

Noble being ! who has died
Like the One we crucified,
Then embalmed and deified :
  Noble brother man !

Great is he as martyrs brave !
Greater, mayhap, for he gave
His loved life to heal and save
  Wounded brother man !

He had only one wide creed :
Love ! that made his warm heart bleed
For a fellow creature's need,
  Noble brother man.

O

O Strange World

In the storm he heard man's moan,
Touched he was with human groan,
Pity made his soul her own,
        Saintly brother man.

Oh ! that all could mount as he
Into Fame unselfishly,
Then would all the wide world be
        Filled with noble man.

Shout his charity abroad,
Ope your hearts and loud applaud
Noble son of nobler Lord,
        Noble fellow man !

O STRANGE WORLD

THOU would'st congeal my warm heart with thy cold,
        O strange World, O strange World !
The sun has gone out of thee and thou art old,
        O strange World, O strange World !
Nobility dies with the gold of thy treason,
And Love lies congealed in the ice of thy reason,
        O strange World, O strange World !

Fresh beauty of feeling thou killest with scorn,
        O strange World, O strange World !
Would'st harden the tenderest heart that is born,
        O strange World, O strange World !
But cultured by sorrow, and strengthened by chiding
Love in each blossom is ever found hiding,
        O strange World, O strange World !

MAN, AN INSTRUMENT USED OR ABUSED

I AM an instrument so fine
That I can see
The sunbeams laughing in the wine
In summer glee,
The small, white flowers that gave the berries birth
And overran with purple bloom the earth
Are plain to me!

2.

So fine am I, I may not be
Abused by one,
Or strange distorted things I see,—
A double sun!
All beauty and sweet poetry are fled,
And I lie vacant with my senses dead,
Of use to none!

THE WAR OF LIFE

1.

TRUMPETS blow, and weapons weld!
I, at Home, am sighing,
For in flowery fetters held
My great soul is dying;

2.

Nature bids me break the mesh
Loving hands are weaving
Round my growing heart of flesh,—
Larger dreams conceiving.

3.

I must go to fight the foe,
Dashing down to battle,
Hear life's dismal wails of woe,
Death's wild arrows rattle.

4.

Never could my soul enlarge
Cramped in this lone valley,
I must hosts of evil charge,
Fainting brothers rally,

5.

Till we reach the mountain cone
Where the Light is shining,
Where a soul, with God, alone,
Stands, Life's dream divining.

THE
BLESSINGS OF FORGETFULNESS

1.

OH ! to throw blinding passions of the Past
Into the gloom,
And peer thy soul into the Future vast
Where Love flowers bloom !

2.

Oh ! to forget when false lips pressed on thine
For thy soul's weal
A kiss that seemed a testament divine,—
Love's warm, red seal,

3.

Broken as lightly as a child at play
Shatters his toy,
Laughing to think it was but yesterday
His only joy !

4.

Oh ! to lose memory of the selfish pride
Of prostrate years,
And feel that all the living moments guide
To higher spheres.

5.

To cast away the gaudy cloak of shame
    That once ye wore,
When thro' Time's dusty cavalcade ye came
    Limp and footsore;

6.

To humbly wear the robe of simple white
    Without a stain,
Woven by Truth upon the Loom of Light
    Thro' hours of pain!

7.

To lose the memory of a cruel word,
    Stiletto-keen,
And live as though the ear had never heard,
    Or eye had seen!

8.

To quite forget the weight of palsied Care
    In regained Youth,
And climb, strong-hearted, to the inspiring air
    On heights of Truth

9.

To burst the bonds of selfish fret and fume
    And fly away
Out of thy conscious atmosphere of gloom
    To golden day!

TO POETRY

1.

OFT have I smiled when little souls have dared
    To body forth thy mind,
As tho' thou could'st be measured or compared,
    Schooled or defined;

2.

In a mute bondage held, or subtly draped
    In syllables or rhymes,
Tortured or cramped, enlarged, or pattern-shaped
    To suit man's times !

3.

Thou who art Spirit !   Not a mortal thing
    Fast bound in fleshly cell,
But an expanding wonder that hath wing
    Before Death's knell

4.

Thou who wilt bless with life the broken phrase
    Born on a feeling tongue,
And hide from Culture, if she scorn to raise
    Song thou hast sung !

RICH AND POOR

THE RICH MAN TO THE POOR MAN

POOR Friend !   Accept this trifle ; may it be
A blessing to thee ; if I gave my all
It might be thine undoing.   Keep thou poor,
And rouse no envy in thy brother's breast.
A touch of tenderness, at sight of thee,
Oft-times would bid me place in trust for all
My worldly riches, but the gift, I feel,
Would yield no common good, and, in the end,
Some crafty soul, what I had lost would gain,
By plundering from the rest.   The rich become
The world's great wealth conservers,—strong trustees.
If I my riches misered, they would melt
Like mountain-snow dissolved by summer sun

'Tis enterprise alone that fosters gold.
The rich man's wealth is pay-roll for the poor.
If in a common "pool" our wealth were stored
All stagnant with corruption it would dry
'Neath thirsty suns.
They say 'tis easier for a camel's bulk
To minimize itself into "the needle's eye"
Than for a wealthy man to enter heaven!
Believe them not . my soul
Has but to knock to gain its heaven! For think!
I trust not in my riches. Back I fling
The mad temptations, that, like flames, would burn
The very vitals of the rich away!
Ah! I know all too well that strength alone
Can gain the promised heritage of man,
Whether we look
For Greek contentment, or the Buddha dream,
Or Christ's divine Hereafter, and I know
The poor, untried by riches, cannot gauge
The burdens and temptations of the rich.
Therefore, be not contemptuous, but be kind.
If your discomforts make you long for bliss,
My beds of comfort only jade my soul.
There is no common joy beneath the blue
Except the glowing dream of what's to come.

RICH AND POOR

THE POOR MAN TO THE RICH MAN

RICH one! I thank thee for thy gift; it means
To me salvation; 'tis as though thy hand
Were Heaven's keen instrument to cut my soul;
For, last night, staring 'neath the silver stars
My parchèd lips cursed God. I said to Him,
The world is wide, but all its riches lie

In Cain's red hand.   Naught but the air is free,
(Save Beauty that the dullest eye may daze!)
E'en thy loved sunset man would fence away,
That he might sell brief peeps of it for gold.
Man guards his wealth much as the serious ape
Pouches his plunder.
                         Tell me, rich one,
Have I done aught to reap this punishment?
No value place I on your reasoning,
For each man builds his own philosophy
To suit his soul.   Why do I starve?   'Tis not
That I refuse to break thy roadway stones
Being lazy ; there are no stones to break : I walk
'Tween flowering hedgerows and the cornfields wave
Their gains in hundred-folds, which thou alone
May gather.   Why thou alone, O rich one?
Are not thy garners full?   Doth not thy land
Languish beneath its own fertility?
And yet I starve   while in thy aproned lap
Thy labour-saving engines pour their gains
Cold comfort is there in a word.   I want,
And I must have ; or starve, and die,
Soiling the virtue of thy wealthy name
In thy sure Heaven.
I know full well thou wert not born unkind,
Thy heart is like mine own, but years of wealth
Have taught no tenderness.   I dare not preach !
If with thy wealth thou dowered me I would laze,
While ye work harder as thy wealth expands.
The modern fabric that doth clothe the world
Is marred with rents, and I am one of them.
Thou canst not patch me, but the day will come
When some divine discoverer shall make
The garment whole.   Meanwhile, for thy kind gift,
Accept again my thanks   But think ! think ! think !
'Tis feeble brotherhood when brothers starve !

YOUTH AND AGE

HEAR me, my little one,
Ere my sun wane,
I am the mountain,
You are the main;
Lightly with life you ride
Tossed on the frothing tide,
I am the eye that looks down on the plain.

Youth is the laughing sea,
Age is the rock,
Made by the storm of years,
Hardened by shock,
Age is the eye that sees
Life's hidden mysteries,
Silver-hairs lighten the path of the flock.

YOUTH AND AGE

YOUTH TO AGE

TRUE, true, dear father mine,
Give my lips power,
You are the grave of Thought,
I am its flower,
I shall bear fruit of you
Nourished by new-born dew,
While a new sun shall new light on me shower.

Youth is the glowing forge,
Age is the hand
Welding the plough of Thought
To delve the land;
Scatter your seed, O Age!
While Youth's spring-tempests rage,
'Neath God's warm sun let the harvest expand.

THE YEARS CREEP ON, THE CRUEL CREEPING YEARS

THE years creep on, the cruel, creeping years ;
  I look upon the sun and it is gone ;
  I mark an inch of Time ; my work is done ;
The years creep on, the cruel, creeping years.

I read their record with an eye of pain
And feel their memory bulk in large disdain,
  Like an embodied Fury armed with lance
  Forged by the wild, untutored hand of Chance ;
The years creep on, the cruel, creeping years.

'Tis vain to bid my fingers wipe away
The inexorable record of my day,
  Vain to bid Memory change her ancient eyes
  And view the Present with a babe's surprise,
The years creep on, the cruel, creeping years.

Vain to hold parley with a heart forlorn
Cut with the weapon of each day's new scorn,
  So from the care-taught footprints of the Past
  I leap with Hope into the unknown Vast,
And leave the years, the cruel, creeping years.

BLIGHTED SPRING

A PICTURE

I.

MOIST was the earth with dew ;
    The Hope-sprung flowers,
Full of the lush, warm blood of new-born June,
    Laughed in their bowers,
    And gently threw
Sweet perfumes o'er the land in unseen showers ;
    While Earth's glad morning-tune

Was carried sky-ward by the circling lark
　　To tell the blue,
The round, red sun had risen from the dark
　　And all was new.

2.

The May-buds laughed again, the daisies smiled,
And with fresh honey lazy bees beguiled;
　　The birch-trees, overjoyed,
　　With the soft breezes toyed,
And shook their dewy garments into rain
　　Upon the sobbing grass,
　　Which looked so green (alas !
No heart could dream 'twould thirst one day in vain,
　　When July burnt earth's crust
　　Into delirious dust !).

3.

The sun peeped o'er a hill, where elm-trees waved
　　With their forked-arms in glee
A nested colony of crows, who craved
　　From earth their morning fee
Of worms, or snails, or dead mortality;
　　And through their hoarse throats cawed,
　　As though the risen world would be o'erawed
　　With their black majesties above,
Sleek,—like funereal mummers,—drunk with Spring-
　　tide love.

4.

　　Below them stood a chapel, over-run
　　　With agèd ivy, teazing waiting Death
　　With new green leaves, on which the crimson sun
　　Shone kindly, while the morning's breath
　　　Whispered a holy prayer
More pure than priest may chant from missal rare.

Above the ancient porch, where Gothic hands
    Had chiselled wonders in the mouldering stone,
A blood-red rose was trained with nails and bands,
    Until into a cross its form had grown ;—
A flowering cross which told men each mid-year
Of bleeding Jesus on his cruel bier,
    An emblem richly blest
With lore of Love breathed from his Sacred Breast.

5.

    High on the soaring spire
A sacred cock was crowing to the morn,
    Telling of Peter's ire
When he denied his Lord with thrice-told scorn ;
    Ah ! woeful tale to tell
Above the wedding-chime or cold, death-bell !
A pious pantomime that warned the bad
But bade the good continue pure and glad.

6.

Beneath its shelving eaves the swallows glued
    Their rounded palaces with mystic skill,
And reared to heaven another tender brood
    Of light-winged Architects to Nature's will.

7.

A rippling river ran fine silver thread
    Through meadow-carpetings of green and gold :
For there the myriad King-cups (fed
    On dew and sun) their eyes would ope and fold,
      Painting with yellow-flood the grassy bed
      Through which the serpentining river led
To where the sea performed in chantings old,
    Sad solemn music to the drownèd dead.

8.

And through this meadow, merry with its morn,
A lonely lady wandered, heart forlorn,
    To cull the sacred flowers
    Fresh from the dewy hours,
Blue-bells and lilies, red-tipped daisies gay,
    Memorial pansies and forget-me-nots,
Hid by the golden buttercups' display
    In choice, remembered spots.

9.

All weary were her eyes and full of tears,—
For Sorrow-frost had nipped her summer years,—
Her hair was dark, her eyes were like the sloe,
Silent interpreters of her heart's woe.
In solemn black she mourned some soul far-fled
    From all these new delights of flower-clad Spring,
For him alone her pearly tears were shed ;
    She would have bribed grim Death that soul to
        bring
Forth from the silent portals of the dead,
    But ah ! she knew 'twere vain
To hope to win from death his greed-got gain.

10.

She bore her flowers o'er the silver stream,
    Past all the maze of buttercups that told
    Their spring-tide ecstasy in flames of gold,
And reached the ivyed chapel's holy dream ;
And o'er her cawed the black, mysterious crows
In darkened utterance which no mercy knows,
And as she passed the portal's red-rose cross
She bowed in reverence on the dewy moss ;
Then to a little grave her feet she led
    And, kneeling, fell
Prone on the grass, where playful lambs had fed,
And there she heaped upon the cherished dead
    The flowers she loved so well.

11.

"Baby," she moaned, "it was not kind to go,
Lone leaving in this theatre of woe
    Thy mother's wounded heart
    That fretted sore to part;
I saw thee gaze at me with eyes so sweet
    When thy pale lips were dumb,
And, as my warm hand touched thy death-chilled feet,
Thy lips seemed formed into a whispered, 'Come'!
How sweet it is to know that some one shares
    His little heart with me,
That a pure, lily angel, unawares,
    Brings me a heavenly fee;
That when I step upon the unseen stairs
    My heart will bound with glee
To know that someone waits,—that someone cares."

12

Through the gnarled elms above, a moaning wind
Came sighing like a stricken soul in pain,
Who, in his tender Spring-time, once, had sinned,
And now, from Winter, craved relief in vain.
A sudden grayness gathered in the sky,
As tho' grim Death with spectral car passed by:
A feathery snow-pall chilled the tender blooms.
Was it cold Winter masquerading Spring,
Soiling with heavy touch her dainty plumes
In giant frolic with so frail a thing?
It was so sudden chill, so weird, so drear,
No eye could gaze abroad without a fear!

13.

The crows' hearts trembled for their rocking nests;
But two red robins from sore-troubled breasts
    Piped two sweet songs
Of mothers' trials and of maidens' wrongs,
And, venturing, touched the prostrate lady's head,
But she heard not their music, she had fled
Up that bright stairway, where her baby led

TO AUTUMN

O DREAMING Autumn, melancholy queen !
Decked with a few stray roses in thy hair,—
Roses which Summer with a kindly care
Budded for thy delight but left unseen ;
What lavish colours now invade thy green,
    What belts of red, what flounce of flaming gold,
    What atmosphere of purple round thee rolled,
While thy blue eyes are dreaming in between !
I know thy thoughts : thou art of Duty tired,
    Tired with thy long attendance on the Sun,
And now thou sittest down to be admired,
    Counting thy jewels from his wooings won ·
I fain would watch thee 'till the snow-fays fall
And steal thee from me 'neath their soft white pall.

THE SWORD'S QUESTION

1.

TELL me who art thou, O Warrior,
    Tell me who art thou ?
Art thou murderous Melancholy
    With a frowning brow,
Or art thou light-handed Folly
    With no sacred vow ?

2.

Or a mighty hero, Warrior,
    For the great world born,
Lonely thinker for the many
    While they pass in scorn
Caring not if there be any
    Threatening Morrow-morn ?

3.

If thou art the world's great hero,
  Warrior, I am thine !
In thy grasp I move as lightly
  As a quill divine,
Wielded tenderly and rightly
  As the Cross I shine !

4.

Use me then with care, O Warrior,
  Use me with sweet care,
For no Murderer's hand intended
  Nor for Folly fair,
With my hero's heart soft blended
  We may slay Despair !

TO THE *HYPOCRITICAL* BOER

DARE you with your deceitful lips
  Invoke the Almighty's name
While with your shifty finger-tips
  You touch the gold of shame ?
And dare you kiss the gentle cheek—
  The soul of Christ—and cry,
"This is the nation that you seek,
  Arise, and crucify ? "

Yes, you have dared ; and now your grave
  Yawns in the Potter's field,
In such a spot a traitorous knave
  May fitly be concealed,
To all your wiles the world is dumb,
  The Universe is hushed,
While marches to the beat of drum
  The brave and gently just.

THE BOER WAR

THE SONG OF THE LOCKSLEY HALL VOLUNTEER

In my heart there rings an echo sounding from the
distant past
As I march with feet of courage to defy the cannon
blast !
Englishmen are proud they tell me !   Justly proud ;
we are no cowards,
We but live to do our duty, emulating Drakes and
Howards.
Not on conquest grows our Empire, but on Justice,
Freedom, Truth,
Coursing through our generous arteries, dowered with
perpetual youth.

Ah ! I know our ruler's virtue, once too tender and
too kind,
Made sublime engagements freely, weakly valiant,
meekly blind,
Would not battle down rebellion but in virtuous
content
Calmed the child that brought the trouble and
refrained from armament :
Now the air is loud with treason and I hear the bugle
calls
Sounding through our Empire palace from our golden
Southern halls,
For the rebel hearts have risen 'gainst the Liberty we
prize
While they thumb with martial fingers Bible-lessons
into lies,
And above the claims of Commerce sounds God's
thundering command,
" Mount the kopjes, storm the trenches, with My
lightning in thy hand ! "

Glowing with unselfish glory all our brave battalions
  march
To defend the Empire fabric at the keystone of the
  arch,
And to plant the flag of Freedom on a new Imperial
  wing
Where a sullen martial people but a feeble Freedom
  sing,
Freedom to debase their brothers, not to blend with
  them and live
Fighting ignorance and folly with Love's proud
  prerogative,
Forth we go! and all the nations know full well we
  bear the gun
Not to boast of new dominion but of Freedom's
  victory won!

THE DYING OTTOMAN

TO THE POETS OF WAR

1.

CRY ye for blood, ye poets of the earth?
  Whose words like flower-lined rivulets should run,
Bright with the passion of their mountain birth
        And full of sun.

2.

Thy tiger tongues, like a wild vulture, scream
  Impatient that the dying is not dead,
While the warm sun of Love, the Christian's dream,
        Shines overhead.

3.

I see armed kings in danger patient stand,
  Watching with anxious eyes the slow decay,
Ready to parcel with a peaceful hand
        But loath to slay

4.

Why write ye words then with a slaughterer's pen
 Dipped in a pool of thy warm brother's blood?
Rolls there no nobler vision 'neath thy ken
    Than this red flood?

5.

Have cultured centuries cultured thee in vain,
 That ye must needs like rude barbarians cry,
Dancing in fury round a heap of slain
    Without a sigh?

6.

Is truth the virtue of a Grecian lip
 Or probity the sweet of Moslem tongue,
That we should let the fearful war-dogs slip
    As ye have sung?

7.

Be silent, while Earth's emperors decree
 To stay the gathering avalanche of wrath,
Lest the warm Orient in the tempest be
    Crushed by the North.

THE EMPIRE PSALM

Moan, moan the dirge of War!
 The brave have gone we loved so well;
 Our hearts were with them when they fell,
 O! cruel glory of the shell!
Moan, moan the dirge of War!

 Moan, also, for our stricken foes,
 For those who lusted for our blows
 And in our valour find repose,
Moan, moan the dirge of War!

Then strike upon a grander string
And sing a song the world may sing ;
Chant, Empire, chant the solemn psalm
And wave the censer and the palm ;
The solemn psalm of Truth and Right
That only Freedom can indite ;
 Chant, chant the Empire Psalm !

Tell of the Empire that expands
Because it puts forth loving hands,
And binds the bad and frees the good,
And homage pays to womanhood ,
 Chant, chant the Empire Psalm !

Chant of our ports we open wide,
Wherein the foreign ships may ride
And furl their sails and feel their pride ;
And chant of Justice to the slave,
Morals that make a country brave,
And Principles that starve a knave ;
 Chant, chant the Empire Psalm !

Chant of the daring of our dead
Who for fair Freedom fought and bled
'Till Freedom crowned our Royal Head,
 Chant, chant the Empire Psalm !

Chant of our Fleet that guards the sea,
And of our Kingship of the Free,—
Edward, the King of Liberty !
And of the century to be
When War shall know no history ;
 Chant, chant the Empire Psalm

Chant of the willing hearts that come
Roused by the magic of our drum

To fend our grand Imperial home ;
Chant 'till each nation shall prolong
The echo of our glowing song ;
    Chant, chant the Empire Psalm !

PEACE !

No more, O land ! let War's loud lion roar,
    But let the lamb of Peace come forth to play
    And with the daffodils make holiday
Now that fair Spring renews her velvet floor,
Let us no idol Victory adore,
    Or fan a bonfire boastful of delight
    If we the victors be in the world's fight,
But let us Love's dominion then restore ;
For in Love's land alone can Beauty live,
    She is elusive as a modest maid,
Like sun-taught flowers her life is fugitive,
    See, how from wintry-war they shrink afraid :
Blow, then, with generous breath thy wrath afar
And send forth Love to snare this lion War.

LOVE POEMS

THE SONG OF THE ROSE-LILY-FAIR

CHANT me the Psalm of the Stars, with thy dark
    voice, O Night!
Open thy casket of gems to my wondering sight;
Spread out thy mantle of velvet, blue as the deep,
And scatter thy diamonds before me, ere I to sleep
Sink in thy warm, summer arms. For 'tis late, 'tis
    late,
And my lover doth tarry, sweet Night, and I wait
Weary with exquisite longing. Sing to me, sing!
If the stars from their vision above can good news of
    him bring,
Bid them in chorus majestical hymn to my ears
Comfort and tender rejoicings, killing my fears.

O! be thou kind, sweetest Night, for I wander alone,
Rose-lily-Fair of the valley, where I am known
To the eyes that are sleeping around me; and O!
Did they feel I were here, on the morrow would
    blow
A biting scandal of wind and a withering frost,
And the Rose-lily-Fair of the vale would be lost! be
    lost!

In my heart I care naught for their scandal; the
    breath
That may blow from the mouths of this village of
    Death

Knows not the inner, sweet feeling that bears me afar
In communion with tongues of the woodland and
thoughts of a star ;
For they have no visions of Love, and feel not the air
Charged with sweet, hidden enchantment, mystical,
rare !

Scandal ! that plucks a pure rose-bud to peer in its
heart,
And, bold with its fingers detective, tears it apart,
And murders itself in the act ; for the rose, Love-
beguiled,
Was pure 'til its meddlesome fingers touched and
defiled !
Scandal ! that smirches a lily with fingers of gall !
Puff ! I would blow it for ever from great and from
small !

But hide me, O Night ! for its tongue is like terrible
fire
That, stirred with the breath of the tempest, roars
higher and higher ;
Dip thy blue mantle deep down in Oblivion's dye,
And wrap me securely, sweet Night, from inquisitive
eye !

Picture my lover, fond Night, with his dark, silken
hair
Carelessly blown into curls, that entice and ensnare
Every fanciful glance of a maid · and remember his
eyes ;
How they blaze like thy diamonds before me, and
scorch and despise
The hatred and arrogance round them. Think of
his brow,
Dark with the depth of his thought, lit with forehead
of snow !

Was there ever a lover more perfect, and gentle, and
  sweet ;
O ! why does he tarry so long when so hurried thy feet?

There's a movement away on the mountain, behold
  a lithe form
Hides for a moment my star.   The fair West is still
  warm
With the heat of the sun-fire descended ; there in its
  gold
I see a dark outline move swiftly, a weird being, bold,
Treading the edge of the world !   It is he ! it is he !
Chant me no psalm of the stars, gracious Night ! for
  I see
The only true soul upon earth who can now sing to me !
Behold ! he descends from the gold to the deeps of
  the Night,
And through mystical darkness draws near, to break
  forth on my sight !

Why comes he o'er mountains of danger, thro'
  depths of despair,
To woo with his breath the Rose-lily he deemeth so
  fair ?
There are thousands more lovely than I, thousands
  that shine
Like the innocent dew-drops of morning, fragrant,
  divine !
Thousands to come at his calling, to wait for his
  word,
Sweeter than strains of emotion from love-throated
  bird.

I knew he would come ! there were whispers of love
  in the breeze,
And my heart felt no portent of sorrow curdle and
  freeze,

236 The Song of the Rose-lily-Fair

Hark! there's a voice in the darkness! It bursts
    into song!
Great spirits that guide us! I pray ye that music
    prolong!

    Float down, song of Love, to my Rose-lily-Fair,
And purl thro' those shells 'neath her gold-streaming
    hair,
        That her heart may rejoice
        At the sound of my voice
As I sing, "I am coming, my Rose-lily-Fair.

"Alone with thy heart, O my Rose-lily-Fair,
    The sorrow and joying of Life I will share,
        Or break at thy shrine
        The casket divine
    That treasures this heart for thee, Rose-lily-Fair!"

How fanciful free is his heart! with what skill he can
    lure
The delicate love of a maid the world's scorn to
    endure!
Lovely enticement of music! If its magic will make
A fluttering feeling of joy in the folds of a snake
How wondrous its thrills in a maiden who lives for
    love's sake!

'Twould be cruel, and wanton, and much over-bold
To say I would barter my love for an image of gold,
But to say I would die for a voice that is tender and
    true,
Would but speak the heart's language, fair maid,
    both for me and for you!
How tenderly sweet the notes die! How his arms
    round me wreathe,
And I hear from his lips a soft word that his soul
    seems to breathe

The Song of the Rose-lily-Fair

The stars like bride-blossoms above; the heart of the
    maid below
Panting and thrilling with love in a bosom of snow.
The minutes speed fast into hours, and the gold of
    the West
Creeps round to the East with a haste no warm heart
    ever guessed
Who has hid with sweet Love in the Night, and been
    deaf to the chimes
Ringing regular beats of the hours in irregular rhymes !
Thrice he tears himself into the darkness, and thrice
    he returns
To weigh me down with soft kisses for which my
    soul yearns,
And thrice he tells me his love, as an angel divine
Will write the decree of his heart on the one sacred
    line
That pledges his name to his Lord. At last his feet go
Out to the uttermost darkness, reluctant, and slow,
And I must creep back with my joy thro' the dim
    purple gloom,
To lay in my white linen nest 'till the rose-sun shall
    bloom.
Happy? Aye, happy for earth-time in love that
    must live
'Till Death, like a tottering beggar, draws near, and
    cries, "Give!"
And then it will pass, like a dream, to the regions
    unknown,
As another new floral-sweet gem for Love's vernal
    Spring throne.

Is that the rain in the valley kissed by the sun of
    gold
Into Noah's fairy-made crescent, pledged at the floods
    of old?

238 The Song of the Rose-lily-Fair

Or is it sedate old Autumn in garments of gold and red
Progressing in pomp thro' the valley to her solemn
  funeral bed?
And why that blast of trumpet that tortures the hills
  afar
In their sacred solitude sleeping, guarded at night by
  my star?
Behold! my small valley seems prancing with men
  on caparisoned steeds,
And spears with pennons are fluttering, restless as
  river-side reeds!
And chariots with gaudy postilions in a sinuous
  cavalcade
Move thro' the village in triumph to the shout of
  man and maid!
And a messenger hurries to tell me, the Lord of
  Gold has come,
With music and trappings resplendent, and noise of
  trumpet and drum!

Why comes he, this over-rich lord, to startle the
  village and me
With thoughts of corruptible wealth, with gold to
  shackle the free?
Scattering his largess abroad like a head of o'er-ripe
  corn
Dropping its hundred-folds round, ere the scythe of
  Death hath shorn!
Rose-lily-Fair must be gracious, e'en as her own fair
  name,
So in garments of white I will deck me to greet this
  Lord of fame.

O! foolish and vain is this village to bow to this
  Lord of gold,
Lured by his pictures poetic to think that a love may
  be sold!

'Twould be vain to apparel in silver a heart that is
    dry as Death
And could never greet his image with Love's poetic
    breath !

Sing me no song of fair gold, O base voice of my
    heart !
Trumpet no falsehood within me, but bid it depart
To the march of the dust of the dead, in velvet and
    plume,
Passing thro' forests of night 'till it die in deep gloom
Banish, O Fancy, for aye from my treasonous sight
This image of gold that shines out like a fancy of
    Light !

Should I walk proudly to meet this magnificent lord ?
Who comes to assault my poor heart with the world's
    magic sword,
As tho' I were citadel easy to enter with stealth
Or to loose its weak gates to the parley of recognised
    wealth.
I, who have looked on the morning with innocent eyes,
And shuddered to see the black falcon dart down
    from the skies !

I have learnt, with bitter sorrow, since my pensive
    life began,
There are deeps in the heart of a woman that cannot
    be fathomed by man,
Deeps that freeze o'er at his coldness, 'till never a
    ripple will play
With the pearly light of laughter on those solid deeps
    all day ,
Yet frozen deeps that will open to the light of Love's
    warm sun
And sparkle and laugh for ever 'till Life's clear tide
    has run ;

And deeps that will change into shallows if he delights
    to see
His bride's light heart as playful as the brook that
    wanders free !

Here comes this Lord to woo me, with a Love-mask
    on his face,
With stately step and bearing,—a not unwelcome
    grace ,—
He lays his lands before me, his hills of gold, his
    dreams ;—
I feel Temptation's luring eye look thro' Love's
    ardent gleams,
I conjure up my loved one who comes by stealth at
    night,
And I place this lord beside him, in all his fancied
    might,
And I scorn this lord's white fingers, made female
    with gems, and go
To the little church of Jesus, hid in the vale below.

My lover's hands are as strong as the cloud-piercing
    hills
That turret the wondering skies with their masterful
    wills :
Safe am I in their keeping, safe, and evermore blest
In the love that has dropt at my feet, like a pillow of
    rest.

Chant me the Psalm of the Lord, O thou silver-
    tongued choir !
Float me on breath of thy music higher and higher !
'Till I touch the kind Ear over all, who will bend to
    my prayer
Tho' I sue Him with cultureless words, that may
    shock His pure air !

The Song of the Rose-lily-Fair

Who can kneel 'neath His heaven and mock Him
    with ready-made phrase,
Who is Lord of the varying moods of the Nights and
    the Days?
Who makes not a rose-leaf alike or a lily the same,
And gives a new form to the cloud, a new shape to
    the flame.
Moods that come o'er us can never be modelled to
    please,
Hearts of emotion are tossed in a turbulent breeze,
And so I will utter the words to the Maker above
That burst from the innermost shrine in my temple
    of Love.

Terribly strong is the tide that o'erwhelmeth my soul,
Great are the breakers that o'er me redundantly roll,
Their music alone I can hear ; the sweet choir is as
    naught,
The prayers of the priest are as sleep that the wakeful
    have sought,
Tho' encircled by tempest-tossed hearts, I, in solitude
    pray
To the God of the Ages who addeth each night to
    each day !

What have I craved, O my soul? May the lips not
    be free
To the Spirit who pours His own life-giving soul into
    me ?
I pleaded the cause of the maid wed to silver and
    gold ;
But I wept for the maiden whose heart for true Love
    had been sold,
And His tears fell in mine ; silent, in silvery streams
Down the cheeks of the Rose-lily-Fair in bright
    diamond gleams.

242 The Song of the Rose-lily-Fair

Sing on, now, O Music ! Intone, now, O delicate
   priest !
Let my soul with thy human emotion have plentiful
   feast
I am once again maid of my feelings, not tempted
   with ease,
Like a thistle-seed hither and thither wooed by the
   breeze,
I will sing with thee now to the Spirit of Infinite
   Good,
Lord of all Sorrow and Joy ; life of all Fire and all
   Flood :—

1.

" Perturbing Spirit of the Deep,
   Lord of the sun and rain,
Wake Thou the sensual World from sleep,
   Stir its great soul with pain,
Then on the tempest-broken sea
Helm thou its course to Victory.

2.

" Let Thy rude wind blow round our soul
   Keen, shivering blasts of care,
Let wayward billows o'er us roll
   And dash us to Despair,
Then calm the wind and still the sea
And buoy us on to Victory.

3.

" Let regal realms of Thought expand,
   New Truths our minds invade,
Dark storms of Doubt blow down the land
   And make the great afraid,
Then in the sunrise let us see
The herald Cross of Victory."

Those words touch my heart ! They are mine, they
are ever more mine !
Break up the icy-rimmed world 'till in flowers it may
shine
'Neath the all-searching sun of great Love ! Let its
thoughts be as gay
As a landscape of meadow-wove flowers in the breast
of fair May,
And O ! when Temptation assaults, I would bid the
World be
True to the teachings of Love, as sweet Love is to me.
Let it listen to voices that speak with the charm of
the flower,
And follow pure Goodness and Truth from sweet hour
to sweet hour,
That no sinister Conscience may rise and with callous
lips say
It deemed the earth-teachings of Night the true voice
of the Day !

Sing me the Hymn of the Sea, O thou mariner blest !
While I wait for my lover to sail to the halls of the
West.
I watch the serpent-like waves curl and break on the
shore
As they shout, like desolate Death,—" I am hungry
for more ! "

Will the sea with its sorrowful breast heave the waves
into foam,
Or quietly breathe in mute rest as we seek our new
home ?
Oh ! I know not nor care ! I will dare the untutored
wild sea,
For the callous old World has been cruel as custom
to me.

244 The Song of the Rose-lily-Fair

To say that she loves me were vain, for she bade the
    love fade
That blushed into bloom on the cheek of the Rose-
    lily maid.
She would bind me in slavery to wealth while the
    sweet eyes above
Scorn her unholy contempt of the Kingdom of Love !

Oh, hard, cold, and vain is her heart, that would
    Nature defy,
Building a Babel of Love 'neath the tender blue sky !
As though Love were a palace of pleasure, with gems
    in the walls,
A cold, cultured heart in the boudoir, and scorn in
    the halls !
Love ! that springs up like a thought, and that buds
    like a flower,
That peeps from a soft-curtained eye in a magical
    hour !
So I leave thee, old World, with the tender-born cry
    of thy young,
The unheeded appeal of the sorrowful Rose-lily's
    tongue.

Be kind to me, Night ! flit not so hurried away,
Lest there flash on the mountains the gold-laced
    skirts of the Day
For I must be safe in the arms of the passionate sea
Ere the old World awake to its folly, its duty, and me.
Our ark of Love, floating in harbour, most petulant
    grown,
Is panting to fly with our souls to wild glories unknown.

Sweet lover, come quickly, why linger so long in
    despair,
With sisters of sorrow soft kissing the curls of thy
    hair ?

To wrench his fond heart from his land is like felling
   a tree
That has woven with mystical loom every Spring,
   with new glee,
Its garment of magical green. But he cometh, old
   World,
And we from the whirl of thy wheel shall be ruthlessly
   hurled :
Too busy wert thou with thy wealth to take heed of a
   girl
Who tried with a love-knot to stay thy mechanical
   whirl ;
As well might a spider's web chain the dread
   sepulchre's yawn,
Or a knight face the arrows of death with a shield of
   fine lawn !

But our new souls are wanted away in the untrodden
   earth,
Where men may think much less of riches, and nothing
   of birth,
Where lordship means noble aspirings, and honour,
   and Truth,
And Love never dies, but lives on in perpetual youth !
O, mariner blest, shall we find such a world with thy
   sails,
Or is it a dream we have wove from a thousand fair
   tales
Tenderly treasured by man ?   Oh no ! we must find !
Or why should it live in the measureless deeps of the
   mind ?

So, blest mariner, sail away ! Bring the gold Book
   of Prayer
Wherein gems of pure English are written with
   tenderest care ;
Then will I after thee say :—" I, Rose-lily-Fair,

Take this love to my husband to have and to hold,
To cherish, and love, and obey him 'till Death make
    me cold,"
And away we will go to the region where Nature takes
    hands
And dances with innocent souls on her unfooted sands,
Where brothers prey not on their brothers, and sisters
    are pure,
And a chastening God makes His Kingdom of Nature
    endure.
Yet each knot, as it parts us, will tie us, I know,
    tighter home,
Wherever your rudder may guide us, wherever we roam.

          Sailor, sail away !
        Lo ! the peaks are lit with fire,
While the valley sleeps enfolded in a warm, white,
    woolly mist,
        But the cross that crowns the spire
Is lifting from the vapour its loved emblem to be kissed.
          Sailor, sail away !

          Sailor, sail away !
       We are fearful of the frost
That is searing all the rose-buds and the lilies of the
    Spring,
        So much lovely life is lost
When the old world frosts the feeling of the young
    hearts when they sing.
          Sailor, sail away !

          Sailor, sail away !
      Where the sun of Love is gay,
Romancing with the roses, not with silver, gold, or pearls,
       But with tender, winning way
Luring Beauty from the innocent, sweet, laughing
    eyes of girls ;
          Sailor, sail away !

Sailor, sail away !
If we linger in this bay
The icy world may freeze us like a limpet to the shore,
And we shall not find a way
To the heart of Nature joying, singing, laughing ever-
more.
Sailor, sail away !

Sailor, sail away !
Raise the anchor, sail away !
There's a little letter lying like a secret in my bed ;
'Tis a great eventful day
And the village mind is stirring with the news that we
have fled.
Sailor, sail away !

Sailor, sail away !
Soon my wedding-bells will play
For the friends of Love will chime them when the
emblem has been kissed ;
Hark ! they clamour down the bay,
And the village, vale and mountain fade away in
tearful mist.
Sailor, sail away !

LOVE HAS COME !

I.

LOVE has come,
Silently as steals the rainbow
O'er the weeping sky,
Beauteously as suppliant roses
Bend to passers by ;
All voices in the air
Speak love to me,
The flowers, Love's priests of prayer,
Pray silently.

2.

And within I feel sweet mingling
  Of a heart with mine.
E'en as sunset flings vermilion
  On the mountain-pine
So two blue-blossomed eyes,
  Bluest of blue,
Bloom on my dreaming mind
  Their heavenly hue.

3.

I am as a rose that blossoms
  In a valley lone
Where a maiden comes to posy
  All the blossoms blown,
For her the buds unborn
  Yearn to appear,
For her the tree lives on
  From year to year.

4.

And the world without now glideth
  O'er my picturing brain
As a thought where she abideth
  Peopling hill and plain ;
She breathes my breath of Time,
  From earth breaks free,
Lifting to the sublime
  The soul in me ;
  Love has come !

TO MAIDEN INNOCENCE

SPIRIT of unconscious grace,
  Purest Love's desire,
All the lilies in thy face,
  All thy rose's fire,
Make a magic in each place,
  And the dead inspire.

Like the bloom upon the rose
  Or the velvet peach,
So the thoughts thy nature knows
  Delicately preach
Homilies the lily blows
  In the baby's reach.

Like a star's intensest white,
  Like the snow's new pall,
As the sunset's dying light
  On the waters fall,
So thy spirit in its flight
  Gently touches all.

"GOOD-BYE"

    "Good-bye! Good-bye!"
Though the morning may come
And the bee for his honey may merrily hum
And the sun to the summer may call,
Yet these words like lead from my tongue must fall,
    "Good-bye! Good-bye!"

    It was but for a day
That your mind like a sun looked into my own
And drew the wild blooms from my bosom of stone,
    Yet you silently stole away.

    "Good-bye! Good-bye!"
    The words are so wise,
They seem to be written like laws in the skies,
    "Good-bye! Good-bye!"

    To see you once more
Would only compel a weak heart to adore
Not you, who art good, but a form that might be
A white lily soiled by rude touches from me!

"Good-bye! Goodbye!"
Though the light from your eye
Has kindled a fire that never shall die,
"Good-bye! Good-bye!"

Who bade you appear?
In your breath there were voices that rarely draw near,
In your eyes there were visions of wonders unknown,
On your lips there were kisses like roses unblown,
"Good-bye! Good-bye!"

I have heard the bell toll
And the muffled drum beat the great march of the soul,
Yet I sooner would fade in the æther and die
Than recall from the silence those words, "Good-bye!"

LOVE, MY GUEST

A GUEST has come!
He burst into my hall of Life as torrid Morn
Leaps with its feet of light upon the mountains
And glides into the valleys 'mid the corn
Waking the prisms in a thousand fountains,
Sudden and all-inspiring did he come.

As wizard eyes read portents of our life
Deep in some magic well,
(If its smooth page be fretted not with strife,)
So he, my Guest,
As Painter, Sculptor, Poet, Minstrel, Priest,
Doth charm my breast;
I would that I with gifted tongue could tell
How his rich art has my soul's wealth increased!

As Painter his conceiving hand will trace
The lore of beauty born in one fair face

Crowned with dark hair, a rose upon her lips
Kissing Love's message from her finger-tips,
And a sweet wealth of violets in her eyes ;
Her neck, (as pure as lilies newly made
By some shy-spirit of a step afraid,)
Light-poising that crowned head as birds poise in the
    skies.
Mark how his touch of beauty speaks
In that rare charm upon her cheeks,—
    That signet mole !
How sweet the emotion of his artist-soul
In that quaint curl escaping from control ;
And how he revels with enrapturing art
Dinting those dainty dimples with his unseen dart,
    'Till not a flaw remains
That is not beautified by his sweet pains !

Then in the sacred niches of my soul
    With Sculptor's art he moulds one figure fair,
And oft he seems a solemn bell to toll
    To bid me worship it in dumb despair :
As in some Time-charmed church the mind may
    feel
    The touch of some mute Presence undefined,
So in the chapel of my soul will steal
    This figure fair by loveliness designed :
Alas ! I think of this fair figure only
And yet it seems apart from me, divinely lonely !

Then, as a Poet, he will weave in words
    These exquisite emotions of my eyes,
'Till, songs as true as those that move the birds
    Into creation from my bosom rise ;

And then as trembling Minstrel of fine sound
    He merges into music and will sing
Notes that upon her lips sweet favour found
    Once when her soul to Heaven rose carolling :

So Fair, So Fond!

Then my fond Guest, like some great Priest in
   tears,
Sobbing sad sounds into impervious ears,
   Leads me to Life's illumined altar-stone
   Where her white hand appears,
By gentle Love impelled to steal into my own ;
   And I seem lost in Light
Behind the curtain of this dark world's night !

Such is my Guest to me, and I to him
Am as a cup wine-purpling to the brim,
   Which he, as Guest,
Drinks as the vital offering of my breast.

SO FAIR, SO FOND!

A Song

   So fair, so fond !
   Your cheeks are the dreams
Of lilies and roses ; and magical gleams
Bloom forth from your eyes as from sunrise Beyond,
   So fair, so fond !

   So fond, so fair !
   No creature withstands
The spirit that moves those red lips and white hands ,
Sweet blossom of Eden entrancing the air,
   So fond, so fair !

   My love, my dear !
   O sing to my ear,
Those songs of your heart that dissolve in a tear,
O sing, and sweet mercy is sure to appear,
   My love, my dear !

O fair as rare !
I look with your eye,
I breathe with you, think with you, dream with your
 sigh,
'Till dressed in your virtue like you I am fair,
  O fair as rare !

  O magic eyes !
 That gaze in my own
And dazzle their splendour around my heart's throne,
Soft, blue curtained chambers where cradled Love
 lies,
  O magic eyes !

  O Lily light !
 O rose of my breast !
With you I would throb thro' this life 'till in rest
We sink in dim dreams on the pillow of night,
  O lily light !

LIFE AND I

My life to me
Is like the sea
Turbulent exceedingly.

And Life and I
Ask never why
A face of tears is in the sky,

Or why heaven smiles
With welcome wiles
To lure us o'er the weary miles.

We pluck the flowers
From Beauty's bowers
As Life and I run through the hours,

254 Had ever Lover a Love like mine ?

Feeling in bliss
Love's passion-kiss
That breathes of other worlds than this.

For Love will find
Another mind
More reasonable, sweet, and blind,

Than our fond own
That feels unknown
On the gold footsteps of Love's throne.

So Life and I
Together cry
There is no grave where Love may lie,

Or why so clear
Should Love appear
A phantom in our atmosphere,

And touch our eyes
With sweet surprise
And raise a thousand longing cries ?

HAD EVER LOVER A LOVE LIKE MINE ?

HAD ever lover a love like mine,
        One half so fair,
        Or fond, or rare ?
O, never had lover a love like mine !

        Millions of maids
        Breathe love in Love's glades,
        And myriads of flowers
        Bloom beauty in bowers,
        But, except for the name,
        There is never a maid or a lily the same,
So never a lover with love like mine !

She beats in my heart,
  Enriches my veins,
Is my sun to Life's chart
  And my star in Night's plains,
In my every part
  A queen-glory she reigns,
O, never had lover a love like mine !

Not her eyes, not her hair,
  Not the form of her face,
But her spirit of prayer,
  Her diversified grace,
Her breath as of summer
  Love-perfumed and warm,
The gentle o'er-comer
  Of winter-wild storm,
Her lightning surprises,
  Her weakness, her might,
Her magic surmises,
  Her fear, her delight,
O these make the joy of a love like mine !

Of a love like mine
To exalt and refine,
A bountiful treasure,
A daintiful pleasure
This ever-unfolding rose-blossom of mine.

Of eyes there are none
That may look at the sun ;
On the light of her mind
I gaze and grow blind,
  But like sunlight in wine
She sparkles within me and makes me divine,
O, never had lover a love like mine !

TO MY LOVE

IF words would bless
I fain would crop men's minds into a wilderness
And at your throne
Present their wordy homage as my own ;
But it would die
As garlands gathered 'neath a rainy sky .
Therefore, my love,
I look in envy on the blue above
And on its page
Would love to write my moral to my age ;
E'en as the clouds
Blot the blue page of heaven with priestly shrouds
And pass away,
So would I love to have my trivial say.
But if the sky
Imprinted my impressions for your eye
Would you be joyed?
Would you not rather be in love employed
And wind with me
The silken Thread of Love's embroidery
'Till the fine skein
Falls tangled in a heap between us twain
And ever more
We strive to lift the tangle from the floor,
While Love stands by,
Alert, with sweet enquiry in each eye?

THE ZEPHYR OF LOVE

A SONG

LIGHTLY she passes along
As a zephyr o'er flowers,
Soft as a nightingale's song
From the dark-breasted hours.

So from my soul, as a breath
From the spirit-world blown,
She scatters my darkness of death
And I see the unknown.

TO MY LOVE

Now will we sit and hear the birdling's praises
Unto the Spring,
And watch the merry, myriad eyes of daisies
Own the sun King.

And we will feel the wind go whispering by
With secrets caught
From fairy flowers, by the lover's eye
With Fancy fraught.

And then will we in Love's pure eyes reflected
See wonders clear
That only by Love's eyes can be detected
And made more dear.

A QUESTION OF LOVE

If a lady's laughing eye
Greet me in a crowd
As a star-divinity
Peepeth from a cloud,
Could I coldly pass her by
With my prudery proud?

Answer, Nature! truly tell,
Could I be demure
If a lovely blue-eyed belle,
Like a snow-flake pure,
In my pilgrim pathway fell
Only to allure?

R

To her blue alluring eye
I would truly say :—
"Blue-belle loveliness! I cry
"Not for floral spray
"But for love that seems to sigh
"All my world away!"

A BACHELOR'S COMPLAINT

1.

THE haunting memory of her voice
My vacant soul enriches
Her pictured images rejoice
My soul's most sacred niches.

2

And yet I am not proud to own
Her entrance to my being,
I fain would rather be alone
And shut my soul from seeing.

3.

Why comes she like a queen to win
My heart for her strong fortress,
Letting rebellious Love come in
As though she were the portress?

4.

I ask the winds the reason why?
I get a sullen answer!
No cultured soldier can reply
Why Life made him a lancer!

5.

And why comes she assaulting me
Armed with her pretty presence,
Making me drink Love's cup in glee,
Love's long rejected essence?

HE CAME AND WENT

HE came!
He touched me with his love,
Took silent soundings of my heart;
I throned him in my heaven above,
I dreamed we could not live apart.

He went!
His melancholy eyes
No virtue found in woman's mart,
My eyes to him were books of lies,
My looks of love,—deceitful art.

And yet my face with tears I line
In placid sorrow day by day,
The thought of him my bread and wine,
And he the East to which I pray.

MY LADY OF BEAUTY

WILL she scorn me, my Lady of Beauty,
If I say to her: "Love, you are fair!"
As I watch the gold sunlight in glory
Descending play with her hair?

Will she deem it a witless emotion,
A conception too palpably plain,
To enter the Magical Presence
Throned in her canopied brain?
Will her fine ear its portals close harshly,
With a pinge of irritant pain?

I could say to the sky-holding mountains,
"Lo! you are high!"
To the clouds as they flit past the eagles,
"How fast you fly!"

Or I might even flatter the flowers,
　　But never could I
Exalt with such language the glory
　　Of earth, or of sea, or of sky :
And how can I praise one so peerless,
　　As though my pre-occupied eyes,
Had suddenly blazed into knowledge
　　Of Beauty in dunceful surprise ?

I have spoken my heart to my lady,
　　I have said : " My Love, you are fair ! "
And my spirit is tenderly conscious,
　　Not of pulseless, dread despair,
But that I am her sensitive mirror
　　Wherein she sees
Reflected her exquisite pleasure
　　Whene'er she please.

LOVE'S RESURRECTION

THOU lovely phantom-presence of my brain,
　　My adoration blest,
Rose of my life with memory's thorn of pain,
　　Rest, rest.

Oh ! when that cruel day
Hid thy fair form away,
Rained on the windows of mine eyes the tears of
　　grief,
　　Loth was my soul to stay ;
I walked the earth a guilty-feeling thief,
　　As though I stole my life,
　　　　And knew not why
Old watchman Death, tired with his daily strife,
　　Still passed me by.

And still is he as busy as of old
Bearing his burdens to the yawning mould,
    Yet leaves he me
Weaving life's fabric with soft skeins from thee.

If I put forth my hand to touch the flowers
    I see thine eyes
Gaze into mine from their entrancing bowers
    With a renewed surprise,
For I remember when thy hand on earth
Woke with a blossom my sweet love to birth.

And if I delve to find
    Riches, and power, and place,
Somewhere in my strange mind
    I find thy lovely face
Brightening my toil, until I see the prize
Become the aspiration of thine eyes.

My memory is dead
To each dull deed born a short hour ago ;
    Life, indolently shed,
Falls like forgotten seed 'mid leaves below ;
    My skies would be as lead
    But that thy form doth shine,
Like a great sun above me, mute, divine.

Yea, I can see thee gazing
    Upward to the Lord,
Standing o'er my Evil
    With thy dainty sword.

And I can feel thee touch me
    With a tender kiss
Thrilling me again, love,
    With a mortal bliss.

I am as a locket
   Cherishing a charm,
Love's sweet pictured presence
   Fending me from harm ;

Lovely little emblem
   Lighting Heaven to me,
Proving Resurrection
   And Eternity !

MY LADY FAIR

   My lady fair !
Love's rose-like blossom, born with lily limbs
   To stray in our sweet air ;
   Picture of reverence rare,
Like a clasped psalter rich with silent hymns,
A warm Aurora glowing in her hair,
Too foul am I to touch a flower so fair.

I should have lived with lilies in the dell
   Far from the realm of Care,
And felt the solemn universal spell
   Of silent stars that tremble in the air ,
I should have wandered hand in hand with night
   And 'mid the silence prayed
'Till some great vision marched into my sight
   And made my soul afraid ;
Then with a hand of holy fear I might
   Have touched my Lady Fair.

How could my lips breathe love to her pure ear?
   'Twould be as though a flame
Passed o'er a blossom playing in the air
   And sullied it with shame ;
Like spring of lion from his cruel lair
   Pawing his dainty game

My Lady Fair

Wanton have been my eyes, wanton my tongue,
    And Vandal-fingers mine,
I have my sister's dismal death-bell rung,
    E'en in the broad sunshine,
And never felt a thrill pass thro' my frame
At the sad resurrection of her name.
    My days of purity are past,
    My innocence has fled,
For me the whirling world goes not too fast,
    I wish the day were dead !

If I could change my wanton eyes and tongue,
    My innocence recall,
If o'er my soul some spirit could be flung
    Like flowers upon a pall,
Then might my dead soul leap to active strife
And storm her with my feelings to Love-life.

    But ah, My Lady Fair !
My lily breathing incense to the air !
    Hope dies in still-born thought,
I cannot change the heart my guilt has wrought ;
The holy halo glorying round thy head
    Bids me not dare
Put forth my soul with innocence to wed.

Like netted bird I live now but to fly
    Afar to spirit-bliss,
Beyond the region of this chrysalis,
To seek the wondrous answer to my " Why ? "
    But my sweet Lady Fair,
She still may breathe her incense to the air
And preach to guilty hearts with her pure eye.

MY LADY FRAIL

SHE was like a heart on fire,
  None could quench her flame,
Burning with a wild desire
  No pure tongue may name ;
She would kiss the lips of praise
  And would flatter gold,
She would barter all her days
    For a deed too bold ;
      Yet she was a dainty thing
      Like a lily in her Spring.

Were there demons in the air
  When this rose was flowered,
Scoffing at a thing so fair,
  So daintily endowered ?
Did the moral current dry
  On the plains of earth
When Creation gliding by
    Made that flower-like birth ?
      Made for us a dainty thing
      Loved of all when in her Spring.

Why stole Vanity and Mirth
  Into her blue eye,
When they pass a maid of worth
  Negligently by ?
Why should she like lightning tear
  Thro' the clouds of storm,
A lovely terror in the air,
    Sin in flowered form ?
      She who was a dainty thing,
      Pure as lilies in her Spring.

Did she meet a heart corrupt,
 And, infected, fell,
Had she with some Mænad supped
 By romantic well?
Crept a poison in her blood
 From some gathered weed
When she wandered by Life's flood,
 No one taking heed?
  She was such a dainty thing,
  Such a loved one in her Spring.

When her beauty fades away,
 When false friends grow cold,
When she feels the living clay
 Tottering back to mould,
When false joy has lived and died
 Need she have a fear,
She who foolishly defied
 Our inhuman sneer?
  What enticed that dainty thing
  To soil the lilies of her Spring?

MAY I CALL MY LOVED ONE "MINE"?

May I call my loved one, "Mine"?
 She who made my fancy run
  Through bewitching mazes,
 And who drew me as the sun
  Draws the eyes of daisies,
May I call her, truly, "Mine"?

Can you tell me, stars divine?
 I have felt the touch of frost
  When the rose was blooming;
 I have seen pure blushes lost
  In a sad entombing;
Were her lips true, stars divine?

When she uttered :—"I am thine,"
Either dimple seemed to smile,
And her lips were parted,
Wondering at her pleasant guile
With a thing soft-hearted ;
May I trust her sweet word,—"Thine"?

YOUNG LOVE'S ETERNITY

1.

WHEN the meadows dream
Of flowers and cream,
And the bees are buzzing for their honey
To the lips of flowers
In the year's new hours,
And the skies find joy in being sunny

2.

Then I roam the land
In my love's linked hand,
And we feel the magic of the morning,
When the birds trill notes
From their trembling throats,
Man's dissonance melodiously scorning.

3.

For 'tis then we feel
The wild fairies steal
On our lips with their blush of red kisses,
And we dream alway
As 'mid flowers we lay
That Love is an eternity of blisses.

4

Can our joy grow less
With mature caress ?

Can our tender souls, united, fly asunder?
Ah! the question dies
In our eyes' surprise,
And the sceptic tongue lies mute in smiles of wonder.

MOTHER! MOTHER!

A MAID'S APPEAL

1.

MOTHER! let your loving fingers
Once more fondle through my hair,
I am sad to see there lingers
In your eyes the glimpse of care ;
Mother! Mother!
Love's warm home within my bosom
Dreads that ghostly guest Despair!

2.

Ah! I see your soft lips quiver,
Smile-waves rippling round them play.
Let them some kind word deliver
That shall drown my fears away ;
Mother! Mother!
Would I were with wings of summer
Like a butterfly made gay!

3.

He would come and flatter, mother,
Flatter with his lips and eyes ,
In his heart was hid another
Secret feeling I despise ;
Mother! Mother!
Would you bend your knees in worship
If your prayers were spoken lies?

4

How then dared he at my altar
Bend, unfeeling, wicked knees,
And with tortuous instinct, falter
Through the heart's wild liturgies ?
Mother ! Mother !
Vain were all his honied whispers
Spoken cold with lips of ease !

5.

Would you take my heart and burn it
In a fierce, white fire of scorn,
And bid Love, the King, return it
Fresh and fair as it was born ?
Mother ! Mother !
If you gave me to his keeping
Sad would be my morrow-morn !

6

So I sighed him 'nay' and wondered
If the hard earth fled in fear,
Or if unseen angels thundered
And from cloud-land shook a tear ;
Mother ! Mother !
Though I trembled with emotion
His calm face was cold and clear !

7.

Cold and clear as are the faces
Hid behind the tradesman's mill,
Counting, valuing, goods and cases
With a mathematic skill,
Mother ! Mother !
Merchandise and I were sisters
To be warehoused at his will !

8.

Mother, it were holier, better
  To be lady of Love's hut,
Than a queen in golden fetter
  Held, if Love's heart-gates are shut;
      Mother! Mother!
Mammon, cold, may purchase Beauty,
  And in peacock plumes may strut,

9.

But he may not buy a true-love
  Though on bended knees he plead;
Love that's true as mine to you, love,
  Flowers to satisfy its need,
      Mother! Mother!
Nature rises in rebellion
  'Gainst all artifice and greed!

10.

Tender love alone shall bind me
  With a cherished chain of flowers,
And the heart of God shall find me
  Buried deep in Love's fond bowers;
      Mother! Mother!
If to Love my soul were traitress
  Thunder-storms would cloud my hours!

11.

And your heart would die in sorrow
  That you had not seen love's tears
As you planned my Life's to-morrow,
  Gazing down the vale of years,
      Mother! Mother!
How can snowy-haired December
  Feel the May-flower's tender fears?

WEDDING BELLS

I.

OH ! my heart with joy is singing
As my wedding-bells are ringing
 Peals of love
  Sounding loud
   In my ears ;
And my rapturous eyes are dreaming
Pleasant pictures gaily gleaming
 In the warmth
  Of the suns
   Of new years !

2.

Not a sad thought comes a-sighing
With those pleasant pictures flying
 Through the gay
  Laughing deeps
   Of my eyes,
Every murmuring note of warning
Those mad, panting bells are scorning ;
 They bring joy,
  Those true bells,
   And no sighs.

3.

But, ah me ! they cease their clamour
And no longer they enamour
 My gay heart
  With their glad
   Throbbing noise ;
Does their silence foretell sorrow
To my lovely, new To-morrow ?
 Oh ! no, no !
  Says my heart
   As it joys.

4.

For again they break forth chiming
With their wild incessant rhyming,
Oh ! sweet Life !
Oh ! bright Hope !
It is plain
Joy has oped its golden fountains
And has levelled low the mountains
Of Despair
Streamed with grief,
Peaked with pain !

5.

And I hear my new name sounding
In the passionate rebounding
Of those bells
As they clang
To the skies ;
Oh ! my heart is filled with wonder
At the mad bells bounding thunder,
Love and I
Are the dream
Of the Wise !

AS DOWN LIFE'S STREAM I FLOW

A MAIDEN'S SONG

1.

MERRILY with my Life I go,
Past wood and meadow gliding,
Merrily sing
My lips of Spring,
Bright Hope my white sails guiding,
As down Life's stream I flow.

2.

To Death the fragrant breezes blow
The misty veil of Sorrow,
Merrily I
Behold the sky
And dream my sunny Morrow,
As down Life's stream I flow

3.

My laughing eyes I see below
Deep in the stream reflected,
And with them too
The heavenly blue
Seem like sweet rhymes connected,
As down Life's stream I flow.

4.

At Night I see the stars aglow
And wonder at their glory,
And back I look
In Adam's book
When Man began his story,
As down Life's stream I flow

5.

But where that heart I seek to know
Who has my own in keeping?
With that Unknown
I'll go alone
To help the world's great reaping,
And down Life's stream we'll flow

THE BALLAD OF THE LILY-WHITE-HAND

1.

OH ! come to me, ye Lily-white-hand
  To smooth my throbbing pillow,
I feel I lie on a bruising strand
  Tossed in the boiling billow.

2.

Oh ! why want I that Lily-white-hand
  To smooth my wakeful pillow?
'Twere best in penance to bid the land
  Wale me with wisp of willow.

3.

Should I steep her deep in grief and groan
  On each betrayed to-morrow
If I made the Lily-white-hand my own
  To touch away my sorrow?

4.

Love says the Lily-white-hand will come,—
  All thoughts of scorn defying—
To warm the heart all chilly and numb
  On Life's rough strand a-dying.

5.

And then my pillow of Life will be
  Smoothed by her hand hereafter,
And she will be as the sun to me
  Or the lily's pleasant laughter.

LILIA

1.

Lilia smiles !
And I am gay ﹒
Miracles are flowered in May
When the fairies light the spray,
And so was Lilia, they say,—
A lovelier blossom far than they,
    Singing to each adorer.

2.

Lilia sighs !
My heart is drear,
Desolate as Death's black bier
Chilling me with passing fear ;
Each cruel sound doth pain my ear,
She cannot know she is so dear
    Or she would sigh no longer.

3.

Lilia dances !
So do eyes
Dazzled with a sweet surprise
When her step with music flies
Light as the clouds that fleck the skies,
As though charmed Ariel might arise
    And set a rose in motion.

4.

Lilia flirts !
And not with me !
I can then a hater be,
Not of her, but him I see
Sullying her with looks too free ,
Lacerating jealousy
    Cuts my soul before her.

5.

Lilia loves !
Ah ! then I lie
In a sweet immensity
Filled with love from her soft eye ;
Measuring quick her deepest sigh
With Pleasure's plummet, knowing why
She sighs to me so dearly.

6.

Lilia fades !
But to my thought
She's lovelier now her hair has caught
The silver that the moon has wrought
Through ages all with Beauty fraught,
And I have never, never sought
To find a lovelier beauty.

7.

Lilia dies !
The air is dumb ;
Consolation cannot come ;
My heart is cold, and drear, and numb,
My grief is heaped in mighty sum,
My soul to Death would now succumb,
No life is left in living.

LONGING FOR REST

1.

Fain would I be a harp in tune
Hid in the leafy trees,
And feel the lulling touch of June
Play slumber-melodies ;
Or fairies from the moon might stray
On the responsive strings,
And with their dainty footsteps play
The heart of fairy things.

2.

Or I would love to hide within
    The bosom of a rose
And watch the bee admittance win
    Droning his honied prose,
For while I breathed its fragrant air
    My loved one might pass by
And place me in her bosom, where
    In breathless love I'd lie.

3.

And then would rest this weary, worn,
    Soft, tender-troubled heart,
That flutters in the wind of scorn,
    And feels the pitted smart
Of looks unkind, of thoughts untrue
    That dart in words from her
Who once to me was as the blue,
    A star-eyed comforter.

WHEN SHE SMILES

1.

WHEN she smiles the daisies ope
    All their laughing eyes,
Brooklets on the mountain slope
    Prattle to the skies,
Birds to visions in the trees
Sing melodious ecstasies
                When she smiles.

2.

Guilty hearts feel sunshine warm
    Thaw their frozen veins,
Heaven wipes away all storm,
    Earth forgets her pains,

Never dares a dastard bold
Bribe a kiss from Love with gold
      When she smiles.

3.

She is sacred as a rose
  Or a violet blue,
Loveliness doth her enclose
  From voluptuous view,
And the very dullest day
Seems alight with magic ray
      When she smiles

4.

But the hill-tops lit with morn
  And the valleys fair
Seem to laugh at me in scorn,
  Stifling me with air,
And the roses seem as lies,
Flirting with their butterflies
      When she frowns !

5.

Therefore pray I for her smile,
  And I'll lightly tread
Over many a weary mile
  Till I join the dead,
For I know the heaven is mine
And I walk with thrill divine
      When she smiles !

WHEN MY LADY SINGS

1.

HANG fresh garlands round the room,
  Open wide the jealous door,
Cleanse the air with sweet perfume,
  High with exaltation soar,

Bid the very gentlest hands
  Lightly touch the tender strings,
For, in joy at Love's commands,
  Hark! my Lady sings!

2.

Hush! ye birds that warble loud
  All your secrets to the trees;
Be as silent as yon cloud
  Floating in the unfelt breeze,
Hold thy breath in loving fear,
  Knowing that an angel brings
Heaven to every listening ear,
  When my Lady sings.

3.

All harsh discords die away
  At the music of her voice,
E'en the very old and gray
  Ope their cold hearts and rejoice,
Thunder-storms of Life are o'er,
  Love has healed Life's wanton stings,
Bold Ambition craves no more
  When my Lady sings.

4.

'Tis as though a light from far
  Fathoms through a sea of strife;
Crystal pure as is a star
  Seem the wondrous depths of Life;
Tangled doubts in twain are cleft,
  Falsehood flies on flurrying wings
Lone with goodness I am left
  When my Lady sings.

TO A HEART SUPPRESSING SWEET LOVE

1.

SPIRIT cold! In folly scorning
    Love's enraptured dream,
Let the melodies of morning,
    Let the singing stream
Woo from you with lips of feeling tender Love's
    esteem

2.

Love lives in the moving millions,
    In the golden light;
When the dazzling star-postilions
    Pass across the night
I behold his chariot moving in the diamond-light.

3.

Like a fire I see him burning
    In my lady's eye,
Hear him speak with tender yearning
    In her quiet sigh,
Ever eloquently pleading if sad grief be nigh.

4.

Love illumes the Book of Ages
    With his magic ray,
Fondling with the well-worn pages
    'Till he smooths away
All the crumbled human story, while he sings his lay.

5.

All the birds in love are calling
    To each other, "Sweet,"
All the buttercups are falling
    At love's daisied feet,
And in Autumn Love's caresses bind the sheaves of
    wheat.

6.

All the lilies of Creation,
   With the love-taught rose,
Smiling, chant in emulation
   Love psalms 'till they close
Life, and lie upon the meadows buried in repose.

7.

Will you let the flower-clad meadows
   Sing while you are dumb,
Will you let despairing shadows
   From cold regions come,
And in winding-sheets enfold you 'till your heart
grows numb?

8.

Pass not by Life's tender sorrows,
   Cold one, pass not by,
But on passion-born to morrows,
   Filled with Man's deep sigh,
Let the poniard breath of feeling draw from you
Love's cry!

SONG

Oh, the breath of my loved one is sweet
   As the scent of the lily or rose,
E'en the violet born at my feet
   No fragrance more delicate knows!

But her words are more sweet than her breath,
   More tenderly sensitive, true,
I would rather one word that she saith
   Than the lordship of stars in the blue!

MY LADY'S HIDDEN SUN

BEHIND the fairy vesture of her face,
    Shedding rich grace,
      There seemed a hidden Sun
That shone through two pure lakes of dreaming blue
    On everyone.

It had an ever-varying magic hue
    Of summer true,
      And raised in me Love's flower,
First the fair blossom, then the full ripe fruit,
    With silent power.

And still it shines in its entrancing way
    From day to day
      'Till in my heart has grown
A tender longing that it fain would shine
    On me alone.

On me alone! Ah! Then 'twould beam so bright
    That every light
      Would die, as star-shine dies,
And I should look alone for my soul's Day
    To her blue eyes.

MY LADY'S LILY

LILY, lit with sacred light,
    Hiding in the grasses,
You become a lovelier sight
    Now my lady passes,

And proclaims you nobly born
    To enhance her beauty,
(As a dew-drop to the morn
    Pays its diamond-duty,)

And she thrones you as a prize
  In her bosom's bower,
Where a thousand longing eyes
  Would usurp your power ;

Or she links you in her hair
  With entwining roses
In a crowning halo where
  Love and light reposes.

Every beauty she re-charms
  By her sweet caresses,
Lily ! Trumpeting alarms
  To a lover's guesses !

LOVE'S PASSION

O Love, why have you whirled my heart
  Into this passion-storm ?
The very world flies past me as a dart,
  My soul delights but in one slender form
And from the commerce of great Life I part.

Fashion and frolic, the recipient sense
  Of sad surrounding minds
    Have now no part in me ;
Helpless I gaze with eyes of eloquence
  At one who gently binds
    My soul,—and laughs at liberty !

You clouds that roll above me with your frowns,
  You varied flowers,
You dulcet dews dissolving on the downs,
  You silent agonizing powers
That blow wild trumpets in my brain !
Have you no solvent for a soul in pain ?

Love's Passion

Ah, no ! Nature but tosses in her nursing arms
    A babe of her own bearing;
My tenderest thrills flush all her cheeks with charms,
    My Love-soul she is sharing !

She on Love's evening all the village lit
    With rose-bloom from the garden of the sun,
And bade a lily through the rose-bloom flit
        Into my glee :
The church upon the hill tolled through its bell
The holy history it has to tell
        Of Love made free,
And in that Angel-lily-one
        Love came to me !

Love, from the earth, broke into purple-bells,
Rambled with roses in romantic dells,
        Shot gladiolus gay
Into vermilion over many a bed
Of blues and yellows delicately wed
        In amorous play;
Murmured in rippling rivulets of song,
    Dashed into torrents with the mountain-rain,
    Caught the wild wind, and in heaven's fairy train
With whip unseen drove forth the starry throng;
Slid in the silent wood with Night, all ear
    To hear the nightingale atune
    His heart unto the melodies of June,
    While I now wander blanching in the moon.

All human hearts like violins are strung;
And yet some blundering fingers oft are flung
    Upon the tender strings ,
They will not play in tune harmonious things.

I struck a discord on her new-strung heart,
I felt the keen discordant part

Shatter the symphony of Life in me,
And now the glittering steel darts from her eye
And stabs my soul with murderous misery.

LOVE'S APPEAL TO NATURE

O BUTTERFLY love !
As you flutter to me
With the delicate touch of your capturing hand !
And your heart flitting out of your eye,
Do you think you can level the pulse of the sea,
Or stay for one moment Time's measuring sand,
Or decorate Truth with a Lie ?
Do you fancy you charm with your fluttering ways
The heart of a man who has measured his days ?

Ah, no !
You may go
With your buoyant display,
With your muslin clairvoying your heart of the air
And your diamond tiara, wealth's crown of despair,
And your lustre that never knows day.

But if you were true,
Like the stars in the blue
And the blossoms I find by the way,
Your blood would impart
A wild pulse to my heart,
In your life I would live and be gay.

MATED BUT LOVELESS

SAID his breath that I was his,
Or that his great heart was mine ?
When he sealed me with a kiss
As a document divine !

I am his I know full well
  By the lashes of the law,
That he's mine I cannot tell,
  All his kisses chill with awe.

Never can he charm his soul
  Like a sunbeam into mine,
Slily, icily he stole
  Like a poison in Love's wine

THE END

Printed in Great Britain
by Amazon